LEARN A LOT WHILE YOU SIT ON THE POT

Fascinating Trivia and Fun Facts About Science, History, Sports, Pop Culture, Technology, Mind Puzzles, and So Much More!

JACK HAYNES

ISBN: 978-1-957590-42-4

For questions, email: Support@AwesomeReads.org

Please consider writing a review!

Just visit: AwesomeReads.org/review

FREE BONUS

SCAN TO GET OUR NEXT BOOK FOR FREE!

TABLE OF CONTENTS

INTRODUCTION

On average, humans will spend 92 days sitting on the toilet over their lifetime. To put this in perspective, that's about one-third of a year in the bathroom relieving yourself. Of course, this average has increased in recent years as more and more people (65 percent) bring their phones to the bathroom, seeking some quiet time to scroll through their social media or read the most up-to-date salacious headlines.

In fact, most people visit the toilet six or seven times a day—and that's when you're still fairly young. As you age, you'll likely find you have to go more often. In any case, everyone spends a lot of time on the toilet; it's something you just can't avoid.

That's where this book comes in. Since the average time spent on the toilet is ten minutes, we've provided you with bite-sized educational (and some not-so-educational) facts that you can read quickly and retain well after you've flushed. These little tidbits will not only make the time you spend in the bathroom more entertaining, but they'll also give you some fun facts to share with your friends—once you've left the bathroom, of course!

While you won't learn enough to get a degree or anything, you'll probably know more than anyone in your social circle about the history of the toilet, bathroom science, animal bathroom habits, and much more! What more could you ask to learn during your ten minutes on the pot?

So, the next time you must go, bring this book along and discover more information than you ever thought you could while sitting on the throne. You'll feel better about spending nearly four months in the bathroom over your lifetime and know more, too!

CHAPTER ONE: SCIENCE IN THE BATHROOM

THE PHYSICS OF FLUSHING

THE GREAT STINK OF 1858

By the end of the 19th century, the Thames River in London was so polluted that overflowing raw sewage led to what would become known as the "Great Stink" of 1858. This smelly situation rendered part of central London uninhabitable. As cholera outbreaks related to the contaminated water further highlighted poor living conditions, a public outcry led the government to commission engineer James Bazalgette to devise a complex new sewer system. This monumental development would eventually be completed in the 1860s and largely suppress waterborne disease. The rapid improvement in Londoners' public health resulted in Bazalgette's model later being used as an exemplar for worldwide public health reforms.

THOMAS CRAPPER'S LEGACY

While Thomas Crapper is often credited with inventing the flushing toilet, this is—unfortunately—a myth. Crapper is associated with several plumbing improvements and inventions, though, including the ballcock, which helped prevent leaks. He also owned a successful plumbing business and advertised the flushing toilet as a necessity in the luxury bathrooms he installed in lavish homes all over Britain. However, Sir John Harington actually invented and patented the first flushing toilet in 1596—240 years before Crapper was even born! So, while you may have always thought you sat on a "Crapper," you're really sitting on a "John."

ANCIENT ROMAN PLUMBING

The engineering achievements of the Romans were truly remarkable. They built the Cloaca Maxima, one of the earliest sewer systems in the world, to channel the city's waste into the Tiber River. In addition, they created aqueducts to transport water across great distances on roads that linked their vast empire together. They built magnificent structures like the Colosseum and Pantheon, incorporating innovative materials and methods like concrete and arches. Their engineering feats significantly improved urban living conditions, leaving a lasting impact on future generations by laying the groundwork for modern infrastructure.

THE SCIENCE BEHIND SOAP & CLEANLINESS

ANTIBACTERIAL VS. REGULAR SOAP

Antibacterial cleansers were created to eliminate or hinder the growth of bacteria, often incorporating chemical substances such as triclosan. While they can be more efficient at reducing bacteria on the skin compared to regular soap, regular soap excels at eliminating germs, grime, and oils. One potential drawback of antibacterial soap is that excessive use may lead to bacterial resistance, which means that, eventually, antibacterial soap will become ineffective. Furthermore, certain chemicals found in cleansers could have health and environmental repercussions. When used with proper handwashing methods, standard soap is typically adequate for daily cleanliness and hygiene.

HAND SANITIZERS

Alcohol-based hand sanitizers contain ethanol or isopropanol, which are effective in eliminating germs. These alcohols work by disrupting the cell membranes of bacteria and altering proteins, ultimately causing the microbes to die. Hand sanitizers typically contain at least 60 percent alcohol, a factor in their ability to effectively combat germs. They've proven to be useful in situations where soap and water aren't accessible. While they may not clean off dirt or grime, hand sanitizers can help you maintain cleanliness when you don't have access to soap and water.

GLOBAL HYGIENE PRACTICES

As you're likely aware, different cultures take different approaches to hygiene. In Japan, for example, ritual bathing in *onsen* (hot springs) and *sento* (public baths) focuses on relaxation and cleanliness. In India, hygiene methods have traditionally involved the use of gram flour, turmeric, and curd for cleansing purposes; however, in recent decades, the use of soap has become widespread. Middle Eastern cultures often opt for *hammams* (Moorish baths) for cleansing and exfoliation. African communities have a centuries-old tradition of using African Black Soap made from plant ash and oils. Of course, in Western nations, the norm is to take daily showers with soap and shampoo.

THE BIOLOGY OF BAD BREATH

WHAT CAUSES BAD BREATH

Bad breath, or "halitosis," is mostly triggered by the presence of bacteria in the mouth. This bacteria breaks down food particles to create sulfur compounds, resulting in that distasteful smell. Poor oral care results in the accumulation of plaque and food particles between the teeth, which makes the problem worse. Foods such as garlic and onions can contribute to stinky breath too, along with habits like smoking and alcohol consumption. Dry mouth, caused by decreased saliva production, can also cause bad breath, as saliva plays a role in cleaning the mouth. Furthermore, dental problems like cavities or gum disease and medical issues like sinus infections or acid reflux can contribute to foul-smelling breath as well.

TOOTHBRUSHING VS. MOUTHWASH

Brushing your teeth and using mouthwash play complementary roles in combatting bad breath. Brushing eliminates food particles from your mouth, fights plaque buildup, and removes bacteria from your teeth and gums. It also cleans your tongue, which plays a further role. Conversely, mouthwash can reach areas that toothbrushes may miss, and its antibacterial properties kill the germs responsible for halitosis. Additionally, mouthwash leaves behind a minty or fresh scent that temporarily covers up bad breath. So, while brushing ensures that your mouth, teeth, and gums are clean and healthy, mouthwash offers an efficient way to freshen your breath quickly. Use both together to keep stinky breath at bay.

TIPS FOR ELIMINATING BAD BREATH

To banish bad breath, make a habit of brushing your teeth twice daily and flossing once daily to keep leftover food from lingering in your mouth and attracting bacteria. Don't forget to brush your tongue—it can also harbor harmful bacteria. Use mouthwash to kill germs and give your mouth a longer-lasting fresh feeling. Additionally, stay hydrated to keep your mouth moist and encourage the production of saliva, nature's natural mouth cleanser. If these tips don't make your bad breath disappear, bring it up during one of your regular visits to the dentist so they can address any underlying problems.

THE MICROBIOME OF YOUR BATHROOM

DIVERSE BACTERIAL COMMUNITIES

Warm and humid, your bathroom provides the perfect environment for microorganisms to thrive. For example, E. coli, transmitted through fecal matter, is commonly found near toilets, and Staphylococcus bacteria can survive for months on surfaces such as countertops and door handles. Molds like Aspergillus and Stachybotrys (black mold) flourish in damp areas like shower tiles and curtains. Fungi, including yeast, also grow well in places that stay wet. The keys to keeping these microorganisms at bay and preventing their potential health hazards are regularly cleaning and properly ventilating your bathroom.

SOURCES OF CONTAMINATION

Microbes find their way into your bathroom through various means. For instance, bacteria such as E. coli can be transferred from your hands to surfaces or through toilet aerosols when flushing. Shed skin cells provide a food source for bacteria like Staphylococcus, which will continue to grow in the damp environment and can survive on surfaces. Water splashing out from sinks and toilets spreads microorganisms onto and across surfaces, aiding their growth. Additionally, mold spores can enter your bathroom through windows or hitch a ride on your clothing or shoes.

HOTSPOTS FOR GERMS

The most bacteria-laden areas in your bathroom are usually the toilet seat, flush handle, and faucet handles. This is because they're the areas most frequently exposed to shedding skin cells and fecal matter. Your toothbrush is also a haven for bacteria, particularly from your mouth. If you don't store your toothbrush far away enough from the toilet, it can also collect undesirable bacteria. Your shower head is a breeding ground for bacteria like Legionella, which loves damp, warm environments. You'll also find colonies of microorganisms on doorknobs and cabinet handles.

THE CHEMISTRY OF TOOTHPASTE & DENTAL CARE

ACTIVE INGREDIENTS

Several ingredients in toothpaste work together to remove plaque, strengthen tooth enamel, and freshen breath. Fluoride strengthens your teeth and prevents cavities, while abrasives like calcium carbonate and silica work to scrub away stains and plaque from your teeth. Other ingredients, like sodium lauryl sulfate, a detergent, create a foam that distributes the paste evenly across your teeth. Choose a toothpaste that's approved by the American

Dental Association to ensure it contains these ingredients to protect your teeth as part of a comprehensive oral hygiene routine.

MECHANISM OF FLUORIDE

Let's look a little closer at fluoride, which strengthens tooth enamel through a process called "remineralization." As you brush your teeth, fluoride interacts with the naturally occurring minerals in your saliva and enamel to form a stronger compound called "fluorapatite." This substance is fortified against acid attacks from the bacteria that create plaque and from the sugars in your food. Fluoride reduces the risk of cavities and can help reverse the early stages of tooth decay by repairing damaged areas too small to see with the naked eye.

TYPES OF TOOTHPASTE

The selection of toothpaste on store shelves can seem overwhelming. Here are some tips to help you choose: Whitening toothpaste usually contains mild abrasives or peroxide to remove stains from your teeth, making your smile nice and bright; toothpaste for sensitive teeth contains potassium nitrate to minimize sensitivity to hot or cold foods; and tartar-control toothpaste, with ingredients such as pyrophosphate, keeps plaque buildup to a minimum. You can also find eco-friendly options with natural ingredients and fewer chemicals. Choose your toothpaste based on your personal oral hygiene needs.

WHY YOUR SKIN WRINKLES IN WATER

EVOLUTIONARY THEORIES

The wrinkling reaction of your skin in water could be related to your evolutionary past. These wrinkles form channels that move water away from your skin to give you a better grip in wet conditions. This improved grip may have helped your ancestors with tasks like foraging in wet environments or navigating slippery surfaces, thereby increasing their odds of survival. This theory is still under investigation, but those annoying skin wrinkles may serve a more practical purpose than you might've thought.

CHAPTER TWO: HISTORY FROM THE LOO

STRANGE HISTORICAL BATHROOM HABITS

MEDIEVAL CHAMBER POTS

Not too long ago, in evolutionary terms, people used chamber pots as toilets—particularly at night. These pots were used to collect human waste, so people didn't have to go to an outdoor toilet. At first, the contents of these pots were thrown out the windows and onto the streets below. While this was primarily done to keep homes clean, it obviously caused unsanitary conditions on the streets. Foul odors became the norm, and disease spread rapidly throughout medieval and early modern cities. Eventually, sanitation reforms led to indoor plumbing, and chamber pots became thankfully obsolete.

ROMAN COMMUNAL LATRINES

In ancient Rome, citizens used communal latrines, both to relieve themselves and socialize. Rows of stone benches with evenly spaced holes overlooked a central waste disposal channel. After going to the bathroom, users would clean themselves with a shared sponge rinsed in salt water or vinegar between uses. This might seem unsanitary by today's standards, but it was a common routine in Roman daily life at that time. The practice shows how the Romans valued communal rituals and their approach to community issues such as public health and sanitation.

VICTORIAN HYGIENE PRACTICES

The Victorian era was filled with peculiar hygiene practices, including the use of "thunderboxes," or wooden chamber pots, that were kept in bedrooms so that people could use them during the night instead of venturing outside. People didn't bathe very often, either, believing that overexposure to water could result in illness. Instead, they relied on sponge baths or only washed their bodies in sections to conserve water. Copious amounts of perfumes and powders were used to mask body odors. These customs may seem odd now, but they reflect the era's limited understanding of germs and the spread of disease.

ORIGINS OF THE MODERN TOILET

INVENTION OF THE FLUSH TOILET

We've already busted the myth that Thomas Crapper invented the flush toilet, but let's go into a little more detail. In the late 16th century, Sir John Harington developed the first flush toilet for Queen Elizabeth I. It featured a water closet and flusher but never became widely adopted until the 19th century when Thomas Crapper significantly improved the design and used his marketing expertise to convince the masses that they needed this device. Together, Harington and Crapper revolutionized sanitation, laying the groundwork for the modern plumbing systems we use today.

TRANSITION FROM OUTHOUSES

In the 19th and 20th centuries, improved understanding of sanitation and hygiene, urbanization, and industrialization spurred a significant shift from outdoor bathrooms to indoor plumbing. Improvements in flush toilets and sewer systems have made indoor plumbing more practical and desirable. At first, only wealthy households could afford indoor plumbing, but eventually, it became a necessity, spreading to the middle and working classes. Indoor plumbing completely transformed living standards, enhancing public health at the same time. People's comfort increased as well, making indoor bathrooms a place where intimate business could be done in private.

IMPACT ON URBAN PLANNING

The advent of modern plumbing enabled cities to grow vertically since buildings could finally be equipped with more than one bathroom. More significantly, modern plumbing allowed for proper waste disposal, which reduced the spread of waterborne diseases such as cholera. Widespread access to clean water for drinking, cooking, and bathing contributed to improved hygiene and overall quality of life. In addition, businesses and people were attracted to urban centers with indoor plumbing, which drove economic growth. Modern plumbing is still a critical aspect of urban infrastructure, continuing to shape cities and protect public health across the globe.

NOTABLE FIGURES & THEIR BATHROOM QUIRKS

NAPOLEON BONAPARTE

The leader of the French military in the early 19th century had an affinity for taking hot baths—so much so that he had his servants add hot water throughout his bath to maintain the proper temperature. Napoleon enjoyed reading the newspaper during his long soaks and—believe it or not—is said to have signed the Louisiana Purchase while taking a bath! His affinity for lingering in the tub was reinforced by his doctor, who recommended hot baths as a treatment for chronic skin rashes. He continued this practice in exile, and in 2021, the copper tub he used during his imprisonment at Saint Helena was even displayed as part of an exhibit in (appropriately) Waterloo.

LYNDON BAINES JOHNSON

Lyndon Baines was the 36th president of the United States, and while he's probably most famous for taking over for John F. Kennedy following Kennedy's assassination, he is also infamous for his unconventional way of conducting White House business. Johnson would often hold meetings or make calls while using the toilet. He believed this was a time-efficient way to multitask, and even though most people saw this practice as odd or even off-putting, it reflected Johnson's pragmatic approach toward governance, prioritizing action and results over formalities. One thing's for sure: He knew how to get things done, even in unconventional settings!

HENNIG BRAND

In 1669, German alchemist Hennig Brand embarked on a bizarre quest to find the philosopher's stone, an alchemical substance many believed would turn base metals into gold and could be used to create an elixir of life. Brand believed that human urine contained vital life essence and, thus, held the key to the philosopher's stone. He collected over 1,500 gallons of urine from himself, his neighbors, and his friends, which he boiled, hoping to extract the elusive ingredient. Of course, that didn't happen; however, in the process, Brand accidentally discovered phosphorus, a glowing mineral now used in everything from fertilizer to steel production.

TOILET-RELATED HISTORICAL ANECDOTES

DEATH OF MICHAEL ANDERSON GODWIN

In 1981, convicted murderer Michael Anderson Godwin was sentenced to the electric chair. However, eight years later, while awaiting execution, the state of South Carolina stayed his fate when it changed its method to lethal injection. Godwin was still on death row in 1989 when he attempted to fix a pair of headphones—while they were attached to his television. Unfortunately, he was sitting on a steel prison toilet at the time, and when he bit into a wire, he electrocuted himself, hinting that perhaps the universe wanted him to die by electricity all along.

FINE FOR NOT FLUSHING

In 2005, Singapore—known for its strict cleanliness standards—implemented a fine for not flushing a public toilet. If you were caught "letting it mellow," you could be fined approximately $110 USD. In 2008, that fine was increased to about $150 USD, and violators could even be subjected to a public caning! The government's goal in imposing this fine was to maintain the city's reputation of pristine streets, underscoring the city's commitment to cleanliness and public health. To this day, these fines deter unsanitary behavior and remind citizens and visitors to uphold proper restroom etiquette.

THE FIRST TOILET ON TELEVISION

In 1957, the television show *Leave It to Beaver* made plumbing history when part of a toilet appeared on television for the first time. While only the toilet tank was shown (when Beaver and his brother Wally used it to hide a pet alligator from their parents), the appearance of any part of a toilet broke social taboos surrounding bathroom privacy. It also signaled a shift toward more realistic television depictions of daily life. It's interesting to note that the network censors showed only the tank because they feared backlash for showing the whole toilet.

CHAPTER THREE: LANGUAGE & LINGUISTICS

ORIGIN OF COMMON IDIOMS & PHRASES

NATURE CALLS

Initially, this phrase referred to needing to go outside to relieve oneself. Even as indoor plumbing became the norm, the phrase endured, and today, the expression is used humorously as a euphemism, signaling the need for a bathroom break.

TAKE A LEAK

As with "nature calls," the phrase "take a leak" hearkens back to the early-to-mid-20th century, essentially implying that you're "leaking" urine from your body. Basically, it means that you have to pee.

POWDER MY NOSE

In the early 20th century, it was considered impolite to openly discuss bodily functions such as urinating or defecating, especially for women. As such, women would excuse themselves in public by saying they needed to "freshen up" or apply powder to their faces. While it's seldom used today, it's still considered a discreet reference to using the toilet.

DROP THE KIDS AT THE POOL

In the late 20th century, people began using the phrase "drop the kids at the pool" as a humorous euphemism for needing to poop. It playfully compares defecating into a toilet with taking children to a swimming pool. Initially, this phrase was used colloquially among friends, but it eventually entered the mainstream language.

WEIRD WORDS FROM AROUND THE WORLD

These untranslatable words have unique meanings and sounds, which contribute to linguistic diversity and reflect the amazing tapestry of human expression. They offer a peek into various cultures and histories, allowing us to celebrate the quirks and intricacies of worldwide languages. Even though these words may sound odd to you, they create a global connection that sparks curiosity and conversation across borders. Slang and untranslatable words help foster understanding between cultures and give us an appreciation for the intricacies of human communication.

Prozvonit (Czech): This word means calling someone on the phone, letting it ring once, and hanging up so they'll call you back.

Tartle (Scottish): This is a term for that awkward moment when you've forgotten someone's name and panic, hesitating before introducing them to someone else.

Kilig (Tagalog): You can use this word to describe that fluttery feeling in your stomach when you start to have romantic feelings about another person.

Abbiocco (Italian): You'll feel this sometimes after you've had a large meal, growing sleepy and contented.

Mokita (Kivila): A fact that everyone knows but won't mention because doing so would cause pain or embarrassment.

Tsundoku (Japanese): If you buy a book and leave it unread, often surrounded by many other unread books, you've committed *tsundoku*.

Uteplis (Norwegian): Literally "outdoor lager," when you sit outside on a gorgeous, sunny day and enjoy a beer, you are *uteplis*.

FUN FACTS ABOUT GRAMMAR & PUNCTUATION

- The formal word for the # sign is "octothorpe."
- Italians refer to the @ sign as a *chiocciolina*, or "little snail."
- Until the printing press was invented, around 1440, most writing did not contain any punctuation; writing was rare, and gestures and voice inflection could adequately convey meaning. It wasn't until the need to organize written language arose (initially to assist with reading aloud) that punctuation became necessary.
- Ancient Romans wrote in all capitals, with no spaces between words. They eventually adopted the practice of putting a dot between words to indicate a break. This practice ultimately evolved into the period.
- The term "comma" comes from the Greek word *komma*, originally a dot used in the middle of a sentence to indicate a short break instead of a long one, indicated by a dot at the end of a sentence. However, the confusion between the two led to the *komma* changing shape to its current form to differentiate it from the period.

LANGUAGE TRIVIA & WORDPLAY

- Approximately every 98 minutes, a new word is entered into the English language.
- "Pneumonoultramicroscopicsilicovolcanoconiosis," a term for lung disease caused by inhaling very fine ash and sand dust, is the longest word in the English language.

- The wordsmith Shakespeare is said to have added 1,700 words to the English language through his plays and poems.
- The word "Hydroxyzine," an antihistamine, and its plural are the only words in the English Scrabble dictionary that include an x, y, and z.
- The average English-speaking person knows between 20,000 and 30,000 words.
- A "pangram" is a sentence that uses every letter of the alphabet at least once. The phrase "The quick brown fox jumps over the lazy dog" is an example of a pangram that was once used to test typewriters because it used every letter on the keyboard.
- An "isogram" is a word in which no letter is repeated. For example, the word "subdermatoglyphic" is an isogram.
- Author Ernest Vincent Wright wrote a 50,000-word novel called Gadsby, in which he intentionally avoided using the letter "e." A text that deliberately avoids one or more letters of the alphabet, such as Wright's novel, is called a "lipogram."
- A "contronym" is a word that is its own opposite. For example, the verb "dust" can mean either to remove or add dust to a surface.
- The word "salary" comes from the Latin word *salarium,* which means "salt money." This word came about because Roman soldiers were given a monthly stipend to buy salt, an essential—and expensive—commodity.
- An "autological" word describes itself. For example, the adjective "short" is short, and "noun" is itself a noun.
- A "capitonym" is a word that changes its meaning (and sometimes pronunciation) when it's capitalized. For instance, the lowercase word "march" means to walk in a measured way, but when capitalized, "March" refers to the month.
- "Mondegreen" is the word for a misheard phrase, often from a song, which creates a new meaning. For example,

people often hear "There's a bathroom on the right" instead of "There's a bad moon on the rise" in the Creedence Clearwater Revival song "Bad Moon Rising."

- Similarly, an "eggcorn" is an altered phrase resulting from misunderstanding what you've heard. An example of this is substituting "for all intensive purposes" for the actual phrase "for all intents and purposes."
- An "oronym" is a string of words that sounds the same as another string of words, such as "ice cream" and "I scream."
- A "malapropism" is the mistaken use of a word in place of a similar-sounding word, often resulting in an unintentionally amusing error—for instance, saying "dance a flamingo" instead of "dance a flamenco."
- A "portmanteau" is a literary device in which two words are combined to make a new word that incorporates both meanings. Examples of portmanteau include "brunch" (breakfast + lunch) and "smog" (smoke + fog).
- When you switch the initial sounds or letters of two or more words in a sentence or phrase, you've committed a "spoonerism," named after a scholar who was famous for making such errors. One example would be if you were accused of "fighting a liar" instead of "lighting a fire."
- Advertisements often use "tautology," or the redundant or repetitive use of words, phrases, or ideas, such as "free gift," "pre-owned," or "advance planning."
- Some languages—such as Silbo Gomero, spoken in the Canary Islands—are entirely whistled.
- A form of English, called "E-Prime," excludes all forms of the verb "to be," designed to encourage more precise and descriptive language.
- An indigenous tribe in Brazil speaks the Pirahã language, which has no words for specific numbers or colors and doesn't use past or future tenses.
- The constructed Toki Pona language has just 120-137 root words and is used to simplify thoughts and promote positive thinking.

- Linguists estimate that a language dies every two weeks, and many endangered languages are spoken by fewer than 1,000 people.
- The most recently discovered language is the Koro language, which is spoken in a remote area of India and was discovered in 2008.

BEST PUNS & WORDPLAY

- I once met a woman who owned a taser. She was stunning!
- When I go golfing, I bring a spare pair of pants in case I get a hole-in-one.
- One time, I gave a performance about puns. Really, though, it was just a play on words.
- What do you call a fish with no eyes? A fsh!
- I once went to a dead battery giveaway because they were free of charge.
- I stepped on a grape the other day, and it let out a little wine.
- My friend became a vegetarian, even after I told him it was a big missed steak.
- My wife swallowed a little food coloring, and she dyed a little inside.
- When I went to the mall last night, I couldn't get on the moving stairs, and I realized my phobia was escalating.
- Speaking of shopping centers, once you've seen one, you've seen a mall.
- I'm reading a book on anti-gravity. It's impossible to put down.
- My mom used to be a baker, but she couldn't make enough dough.
- Time flies like an arrow. Fruit flies like a banana.
- I asked my friend to help me locate my watch, but she couldn't find the time.
- No matter how much you push the envelope, it will always remain stationary.
- I wrote a song about tortillas—well, it's actually more of a wrap.

- The mathematician's bakery was famous for its pi.
- Why don't scientists trust atoms? Because they make up everything.
- Did you hear about the guy who lost his left arm and leg in a car crash? He's all right now.
- The scarecrow won an award for being outstanding in his field.
- I don't trust acupuncturists—they're backstabbers.
- My friend went to a seafood-themed club the other night. He pulled a mussel while dancing.
- The future, the present, and the past walked into a bar; things got a little tense.
- My father used to be a banker, but he lost interest.
- The guy who invented throat lozenges died last week. There was no coffin at the funeral.
- I told my wife she was drawing her eyebrows too high. She looked surprised.
- Did you hear about the cheese factory that exploded? There was nothing left but de-brie.
- My friend plays piano by ear, but I find it much easier to play with my hands.
- My cousin got fired from his job at the calendar factory because he took a day off.
- I went on an all-almond diet once, but it was just nuts.
- My grandmother made me a belt out of watches. It was just a waist of time.
- How do you organize a space party? You planet!
- Teachers are big fans of whiteboards—they're remarkable.
- I just learned that the man who invented Velcro died. RIP.
- There was once a man who survived both mustard gas and pepper spray. He became a seasoned veteran.
- My son says he's friends with only 25 letters of the alphabet. He doesn't know y.
- I told my wife to embrace her mistakes, and she gave me a hug.

- Why don't skeletons fight each other? They don't have the guts.
- What do you call fake spaghetti? An im-pasta.
- Parallel lines have so much in common; it's such a shame they'll never meet.
- Why did the math book look sad? It had too many problems.
- When the electricity went out at the school, the students were de-lighted.
- The shovel was a groundbreaking invention.
- My daughter said that, after she ate her alphabet soup, she had a vowel movement.
- I've discovered that where there's a will, there's a relative.
- It's been a terrible winter for Humpty Dumpty, but don't be too sad for him—he had a great fall.
- Did you hear about the toilet that was stolen from the police department? The cops have nothing to go on.
- Don't let anyone call you average. That's just mean.

CHAPTER FOUR: NATURE CALLS

WEIRD ANIMAL BATHROOM HABITS

DUNG BEETLES

Dung beetles use their powerful legs to roll balls of dung to create nesting material and keep them for future food use. Male dung beetles frequently have fierce battles with each other over the best dung balls, and females carefully build underground burrows to store their precious dung balls. Some dung beetle species even have an innate ability to roll their dung balls away from other beetles in a straight line to avoid having them stolen! Dung beetles and their strange bathroom habits actually play an important role in ecosystem health and nutrient recycling.

WOMBATS

These quirky marsupials have cube-shaped poo, which they use strategically to mark their territory. They're the only animal in the world that poops in cubes. Since their poop isn't round, their droppings don't roll away, effectively creating distinct territorial boundaries. Wombats will leave their cubes on elevated surfaces like rocks and logs to make sure other animals find them. They also use their scat to communicate their presence and dominance to other wombats. Their unusual bathroom behaviors show how wombats have adapted to survive in a competitive world.

OTHER ANIMALS

Sloths, rabbits, and hippos are among the many animals that exhibit odd bathroom behaviors. Sloths descend from trees just once a week to defecate, fertilizing the trees they live in. It's the perfect symbiotic relationship! Rabbits consume their own feces in a practice called "coprophagy," extracting essential nutrients they can only get by eating food that has already passed through their digestive system. Hippos spread their feces with their tails to mark their territory and communicate with other hippos. It's their way of spreading their scent, asserting dominance, and keeping rival hippos away.

BIZARRE PLANTS & THEIR USES

CORPSE FLOWER

The *Amorphophallus titanum,* commonly known as the "corpse flower," is known for its massive size and foul odor, which resembles the smell of rotting flesh. This tropical plant is native to Sumatra, Indonesia, and can grow to over ten feet tall. The stinky smell attracts pollinators such as flies and carrion beetles, who are drawn to the odor of decay. Corpse flowers only bloom once every decade or so, and the blossom only lasts a few days. Despite the corpse flower's smell, its unusual characteristics captivate both scientists and the general public, with people standing in line for hours to witness a bloom.

VENUS FLYTRAP

A carnivorous subtropical plant native to the southeastern United States, the Venus flytrap has distinctive hinged leaves lined with hair-like triggers. If an insect or spider touches these hairs twice within about twenty seconds, the leaves snap shut, entrapping the prey. The plant then uses digestive enzymes to break down its food and absorb the nutrients. The Venus flytrap is an excellent example of an organism's ability to adapt to its environment, as the plant developed its unique eating habits to survive in nutrient-poor soil. While the Venus flytrap looks menacing, it's a favorite among botanists and plant enthusiasts.

OTHER BIZARRE PLANTS

Among other bizarre plants are the pitcher plant, the *Rafflesia arnoldii,* and lithops. The pitcher plant's leaves resemble deep pitchers and contain digestive fluids. Insects are drawn to the plant's nectar, fall into the fluids, and can't escape. The *Rafflesia arnoldii* is native to Southeast Asia and produces the world's largest-known flower, spanning up to three feet. Like *Amorphophallus titanum*, this plant also exhibits an intensely unpleasant odor that attracts carrion flies for pollination. The Lithops, or "living stone," is a succulent native to southern Africa that resembles pebbles, disguising it from hungry herbivores.

ODDITIES FROM THE NATURAL WORLD

BIOLUMINESCENT ORGANISMS

Bioluminescent organisms like fireflies, anglerfish, and marine plankton produce light through chemical reactions inside their bodies. Fireflies use the light to attract mates, anglerfish use it to lure in prey, and plankton use it to deter predators. Other reasons for bioluminescence in organisms include hunting, camouflage, and confusing predators. Bioluminescence is a result of the reaction between the molecule luciferin and the enzyme luciferase. When many bioluminescent organisms are in a single location, they can create a stunning light display that humans find fascinating. During past wars, planes frequently used bioluminescence in the ocean as a guide, allowing them to turn off their instruments and lights to remain undetectable from the ground.

GIANT FUNGI

The largest-known species of fungi is the honey fungus (*Armillaria solidipes*), which grows extensively underground. In fact, one honey fungus in Oregon spans an estimated 2,200 acres! The beefsteak fungus (*Fistulina hepatica*), another giant fungus, is known for its resemblance to raw meat. These fungi play an important role in ecosystems, decomposing organic matter, recycling nutrients, and forming symbiotic relationships with plants. Other giant fungi, such as the giant puffball (*Calvatia gigantea*), are edible and are considered culinary delights. The reishi fungus (*Ganoderma lucidum*) and others are used for medicinal purposes, particularly in areas of the world where traditional medicine is still practiced.

OTHER NATURAL ODDITIES

The natural world is full of other oddities that showcase the incredible diversity and adaptability of life on Earth. Take the axolotl (*Ambystoma mexicanum*), for example, a type of salamander that never evolved past its larval state, reaching adulthood without undergoing metamorphosis. It has gills instead of lungs and can regenerate lost limbs. The aye-aye, a nocturnal lemur native to Madagascar, possesses an elongated middle finger that allows it to extract insects from trees. The mantis shrimp has a punch that would knock out any professional boxer, which it uses to crack shells and stun prey with its strong, club-like appendages. The mantis shrimp can also see in twelve color channels—an amazing number when you consider that humans can only see in three!

ENVIRONMENTAL FUN FACTS

CARBON SEQUESTRATION

In the natural world, forests act as major carbon sinks, absorbing CO2 during photosynthesis and storing it in their biomass. This is known as "carbon sequestration." Oceans also sequester carbon in massive amounts because phytoplankton absorb CO2 and sink to the ocean floor when they die. To fight climate change, scientists have developed techniques like direct air capture, which mimics forest and ocean carbon sequestration to remove excess carbon from the atmosphere, using machines to extract CO2 from the air and store it underground.

RENEWABLE ENERGY SOURCES

You're probably aware of several renewable energy sources, such as solar power, which harnesses the power of the sun to create electricity, and wind power, which converts the kinetic energy of wind to electricity. However, other types of renewable energy sources offer potential alternatives to fossil fuels, as well. These sources include hydropower, one of the oldest power sources, which uses flowing water and dams to create energy; geothermal energy, which taps into the Earth's internal heat; and biomass energy, which comes from organic materials such as agricultural crops, waste, and wood. All renewable energy is clean, reducing greenhouse gasses, and is becoming increasingly more accessible and affordable.

OTHER ENVIRONMENTAL FUN FACTS

Some other interesting environmental facts you may not know include that trees can communicate with each other through a network of underground fungi. This network is informally called the "Wood Wide Web" and shares nutrients and information about their environment. Another fun fact is that Antarctica is a desert, though it isn't hot like most deserts—it's the driest continent, with very little annual precipitation. Also, did you know that a single mature oak tree can host more than 500 different species? It's basically an entire world unto itself!

CHAPTER FIVE: FOOD FOR THOUGHT

SURPRISING FOOD FACTS

HONEY NEVER SPOILS

The low water content of honey creates an environment that prohibits the growth of bacteria and mold. It also has a high acidity content, preventing the growth of other types of microorganisms. Moreover, honeybees add glucose oxidase to the honey, which creates hydrogen peroxide—an antibacterial agent. Together, these factors create a natural preservative, keeping honey from spoiling. In fact, archaeologists have discovered stores of honey in ancient Egyptian tombs full of still-edible honey!

CHOCOLATE AS CURRENCY

Chocolate is a beloved, sweet treat in modern society, but at one point in history, chocolate was even more highly valued—so much so, that it was actually used as currency! Specifically, the Aztecs and Mayans traded cacao beans for goods and services in ancient Mesoamerica. Cacao beans were so valuable that they were used to purchase food and clothing. Some people even used them to pay their taxes!

SPAM

In 1937, Hormel Foods introduced Spam, a canned meat product whose name is a portmanteau of "spiced ham." Easy to transport and with a long shelf life, it became a staple of the American military. Eventually, Spam became popular in everyday households, particularly in the Philippines, Guam, and Hawaii. It has simple ingredients: pork, ham, salt, water, potato starch, sugar, and sodium nitrate, which has made it a convenient meal option for millions of people worldwide. Despite the humorous myth that "SPAM" stands for Scientifically Processed Animal Matter, more than eight billion cans have been sold in 44 countries.

CAESAR SALAD

Surprisingly, so-called "Caesar" salad was not invented anywhere near Rome! It was first served in 1924 in Tijuana, Mexico, when Caesar Cardini, owner of the Hotel Caesar, wanted to make dinner for friends but didn't have much at hand. He tossed lettuce in a bowl and made a dressing from ingredients he had in his pantry. The rest, as they say, is salad history.

OREOS

Looking for a vegan treat that you don't have to prepare yourself or spend a fortune on? Look no further than Oreos! These iconic cookies debuted in 1912 and have been called "accidentally vegan" because it wasn't an intentional choice during its creation. No one predicted that it would end up as a selling point in the future. Of course, you can dip your Oreos in milk, but if you eat them as-is, they're vegan-friendly.

WATERMELON VS. CUCUMBER

Despite the name "watermelon," this fruit actually contains less water than cucumber. There's not a huge difference—with watermelon containing 92 percent water and cucumber 95 percent—but it's interesting to note that something with the word "water" in its name doesn't contain the most water! Cucumbers contain about the same amount of water as both lettuce and celery. All four foods are good for you, though.

BANANA FACTS

Bananas are so fascinating that they get their own fun fact section! They're believed to be the world's oldest fruit at more than 10,000 years old. This is five times older than the Colosseum in Italy, which is only 2,000 years old. Bananas contain 75 percent water and can actually float. They offer the best fruit source of vitamin B6, known to improve brain processes, boost immunity, and restore tired muscle tissue. You can use banana peels to relieve the itching from mosquito bites, too!

CILANTRO

Cilantro is also known as coriander, and some people possess a gene that makes it taste like soap. It contains some of the same aldehydes found in detergents, lotions, and, yes, soap, but some people can only taste the soap. These cilantro haters also share a specific group of olfactory receptor genes called OR6A2, which allows them to identify the smell of aldehyde chemicals in cilantro.

POUND CAKE

Despite its name, pound cake doesn't actually weigh a pound. However, when the cake was first invented in Northern Europe in the early 18th century, the recipe called for a pound each of butter, sugar, eggs, and flour. This recipe first appeared in Hannah Glasse's The Art of Cookery Made Plain and Easy in 1747. The large quantities of ingredients and the lack of leveling created a dense cake perfect for large gatherings, as a small serving would be enough to fill people up.

FIGS

Even though figs are plants, they may not be vegan. This is because female wasps crawl inside figs to lay their eggs as part of the pollination process. The female wasps die during the process and then become a part of the fig, which eventually digests the wasp using an enzyme called ficin, leaving no trace behind when the fruit is ready to eat.

STRANGE EATING HABITS

INSECT CONSUMPTION

In countries such as Thailand, Cambodia, and Vietnam, eating insects is considered a common way to get all the nutrition a body needs. Not only do these countries feature insects like crickets, silkworm larvae, and grasshoppers in their cuisine, but they're also often fried and seasoned to be enjoyed as protein-rich snacks. This isn't the only place where insects find the dinner plate, though; in Mexico, you might discover grasshoppers in your tacos, while in Africa, you can order mopane worms as a delicacy at many fancy restaurants.

FERMENTED SHARK

Speaking of delicacies, in Iceland, fermented shark, or *Hákarl*, is a popular indulgence. For hundreds of years, Icelanders have fermented the Greenland shark to preserve the meat and make it safe to eat. This particular species of shark is toxic to humans when fresh because of high levels of trimethylamine oxide and urea. Shark hunters gut and behead the sharks, bury them in gravel for several months, then hang them to dry for several additional months. The resulting pungent, ammonia-rich flavor is an acquired taste, but Icelanders love it so much that it's considered a major part of their midwinter festival, *Þorrablót*.

FOOD-RELATED MYTHS DEBUNKED

CARROTS IMPROVE NIGHT VISION

When you were younger, your parents probably told you to eat your carrots to improve your night vision. Unfortunately, they were just trying to get you to eat your vegetables because, even though carrots have high levels of vitamin A—which is necessary for eye health—you aren't going to get superior night vision by eating them. This myth came about in World War II when the British spread the story that their pilots were so successful in nighttime air battles because they ate bundles of carrots. However, the truth was that the British had invented radar technology, allowing them to detect enemy aircraft in the dark.

SPINACH AS A SUPER IRON SOURCE

As a child, you may have watched the cartoon Popeye and thought that, if you ate as much spinach as he did, you'd build your muscles thanks to all that iron. Sadly, while spinach is an excellent source of antioxidants and is very nutritious, it doesn't contain nearly the amount of iron most people think it does. This myth resulted from a 19th-century decimal point error that exaggerated spinach's iron content by ten times. Moreover, spinach contains oxalic acid, which binds to iron, making it difficult for the body to absorb. So, not only is spinach not a superior iron source, but the body can't even use most of what it does have!

THE MOST IMPORTANT MEAL OF THE DAY

The first food you eat is technically breakfast, as you're breaking your overnight fast, but there's no specific magic about the meal we commonly eat in the morning. It can provide essential nutrients and energy when you first get up for the day, but not everyone feels hungry in the morning or benefits equally from breakfast. In fact, some people choose to delay their first meal in a process called "intermittent fasting," which actually can stabilize blood sugar levels.

ADDING SALT MAKES WATER BOIL FASTER

When boiling water, people often add about a teaspoon of salt to their pot of water, thinking it will make the water boil more quickly. However, experiments have proven that the tiny amount of salt usually put into the water won't have a tangible effect on how quickly the water boils. To make a substantial difference in boiling time, the pot of water would have to contain 20 percent salt. This would give the water a lower heat capacity than plain water, heating it over 25 times faster, but—and this is a big one—the water would be so salty as to make any food cooked in it inedible!

TOSS FOOD AFTER THE EXPIRATION DATE

The expiration date on food isn't a magic deadline on which the food will instantly turn bad. That date is only used for stores and manufacturers as the last date they'll guarantee the product will stay good. Most foods last well beyond the expiration date, and some foods (canned and other dry goods) can be stored indefinitely and are still perfectly fine to eat. You must use your own judgment once the expiration date has passed to determine whether the product is still good, which means using your senses to decide whether or not you should eat it. In other words, don't throw something away just because it's slightly past its expiration date. It could be a waste of good food!

FOOD HISTORY & TRIVIA

ORIGIN OF PIZZA

While pizza-like dishes can be traced back to ancient civilizations like the Romans, Greeks, and Egyptians in the form of baked flatbreads with toppings, the modern pizza got its start in Naples, Italy, in the late 1800s. At the time, Neapolitan pizza, topped with tomatoes, cheese, olive oil, and occasionally anchovies, was a cheap and convenient meal for the city's working class. Italian immigrants brought their pizza recipes to the New World in 1905, where it became and stayed immensely popular.

HISTORY OF CHOCOLATE

Just like the candy itself, the history of chocolate is rich and decadent. Chocolate first came on the scene in Mesoamerica, where the Olmecs, Aztecs, and Mayans used cacao beans to make a bitter drink for medicinal and ritualistic purposes. Spanish explorers brought cacao back to Europe in the 1500s, where sugar was added to lessen the bitterness, transforming it into the delicious, sweet treat we still enjoy today. Chocolate bars and other confections showed up in the 19th century as advancements in processing allowed for the bulk creation of chocolates for mass sales.

THE PERFECT CHICKEN

In 1948, Howard C. Pierce, poultry research director for A&P grocery stores, conducted a contest to create the perfect chicken, with a turkey-like breast that could feed an entire family. Basically, he wanted to crossbreed different chickens until he found one that consumers would buy to feed their families. The contest lasted three years, as breeders across the United States worked to find the ideal combination of chickens to create the "Chicken of Tomorrow." Charles Vantress, who crossed a New Hampshire chicken with a Cornish hen, won the contest and dramatically changed the chicken species. The contest also meant that each chicken farm created their own "brand" of chicken based on their crossbreeding techniques—brands that are still in production today.

HISTORY OF POPSICLES

Many great inventions throughout history were due to happy accidents, and popsicles are no exception! In 1905, an 11-year-old boy named Frank Epperson made himself a soft drink in a cup, using a stirring stick to mix in the soda water. Then, Epperson got distracted and left his drink outside overnight. The next morning, the drink had frozen solid with the stick poking out. He found that the stick made a great handle to hold onto while he ate the frozen treat. In 1923, Epperson patented his "ice on a stick," calling the product "Epsicles." When his own children began calling them "Pop's 'sicles," he changed the name, and they became the icy treat we still know today.

HISTORY OF THE ICE CREAM CONE

During the 1904 World's Fair in St. Louis, the weather was so hot that Arnold Fornachou, an ice cream vendor, couldn't keep up with customer demand for his refreshing product and ran out of the paper cups he was serving it in. A nearby vendor, Ernest Hamwi, was having the opposite issue: His waffle-like pastry, called "zalabia," wasn't selling well at all, probably because of the heat. Hamwi gave some of his waffles to Fornachou, who rolled them up to serve his ice cream in, and the combination was a hit.

Since then, ice cream and cones have gone together like peanut butter and jelly.

Since then, ice cream and cones have gone together like peanut butter and jelly.

CHAPTER SIX: ARTS & ENTERTAINMENT

UNUSUAL FACTS ABOUT FAMOUS ARTISTS

VAN GOGH'S EAR INCIDENT

In one of art history's most intriguing stories, painter Vincent van Gogh got into an argument with fellow artist Paul Gauguin in December 1888. Afterward, van Gogh, who was suffering from depression and likely other mental illnesses, cut off part of his left ear. He wrapped the section of his ear in cloth and supposedly gave it to a woman at a nearby house of ill repute. We can't know the reasons behind van Gogh's dramatic actions for sure, but historians suspect they weren't even clear to van Gogh himself. However, his troubled relationship with Gaugin, combined with his mental health issues, is most often cited.

PICASSO'S FULL NAME

Picasso is one of the most famous artists in history, but few people know that his full baptismal name was Pablo Diego José Francisco de Paula Juan Nepomuceno Crispín Crispiniano María de los Remedios de la Santísima Trinidad Ruiz Picasso. Each of Picasso's names had specific significance, from Pablo (after his paternal uncle) to Crispín Crispiniano (after two shoemaker saints whose feast days coincide with the artist's date of birth.) His last two names, Ruiz and Picasso, were his father's and mother's surnames, respectively. Initially, Picasso signed his work "P. Ruiz," then switched to "P.R. Picasso" (ostensibly to distinguish himself, rather than as a rejection of his father), but eventually settled on simply "Picasso"—the name we're most familiar with today.

CLAUDE MONET WAS COLOR BLIND

French impressionist artist Claude Monet is well-known, especially for a series of paintings he completed in his later years, notable for their blue colors. In fact, the time frame during which he produced these paintings is called his "blue period." While one popular myth says that Monet was merely experimenting with the color blue in these paintings, but the truth is that he could only see the color blue following surgery to correct cataracts in his eyes. In 1924, Monet told his physician, "I see blue. I no longer see red or yellow. This annoys me terribly because I know these colors exist. It's filthy. It's disgusting. I see nothing but blue." Monet actually wanted to destroy these paintings, but it's a good thing he didn't—to this day, his blue paintings are considered some of his finest work.

LEONARDO DA VINCI MAY HAVE HAD ADHD

One of the most famous artists of all time, Leonardo da Vinci is largely considered to have been a genius. Ironically, during his time, he frustrated aides and assistants because he could never focus on anything for very long. If ADHD had been recognized around the 15th century, da Vinci may have been the first to be diagnosed. He left hundreds of works unfinished, and even his most famous pieces took much longer than they should have. It took da Vinci fourteen years to complete the Mona Lisa, a relatively small painting. Similarly, da Vinci spent three years to complete The Last Supper; as the legend goes, he only finished it because his benefactor threatened to stop paying him!

DALÍ BELIEVED HE WAS HIS DEAD BROTHER

Salvador Dalí's brother died nine months before the famous artist was born. Nine months later, his parents decided to name their new son Salvador, as well. When the younger Salvador was five years old, his parents took him to his brother's grave and told him that he was the reincarnation of his brother. Dalí came to accept this story as true, firmly believing he was his reincarnated sibling. He even created a series of works featuring his older brother, including Portrait of My Dead Brother, painted in 1963.

BEHIND-THE-SCENES STORIES FROM THE SCREEN

SECRET CAMEOS IN *STAR WARS*

George Lucas, the iconic filmmaker behind the *Star Wars* franchise, enjoyed inserting secret cameos in his movies as fun Easter eggs for audiences. For instance, Director Steven Spielberg had placed the *Star Wars* character Yoda in his 1982 film *E.T. the Extra-Terrestrial,* so Lucas decided to repay the favor in *Episode I: The Phantom Menace,* planting E.T. in the Galactic Senate. Celebrities such as Daniel Craig (as a Stormtrooper), Simon Pegg (Unkar Plutt), Keira Knightley (Sabe, Queen Amidala's handmaiden), Warwick Davis (Wicket the Ewok), and Samuel L. Jackson (Jedi Master Mace Windu) also made famous appearances in various *Star Wars* films.

UNEXPECTED ACCIDENTS IN FAMOUS SCENES

Perhaps the most infamous accident in a movie scene is the recent Alec Baldwin shooting of cinematographer Halyna Hutchins on the set of *Rust,* but there have been less deadly accidents during the filming of other movies. For instance, Viggo Mortensen broke two toes when he kicked a helmet during a scene in *The Lord of the Rings: The Two Towers.* In *Raiders of the Lost Ark,* Harrison Ford was ill during a lengthy fight scene, so he improvised shooting his opponent instead of engaging in a sword fight, which would have required much more energy. In both cases, these accidents became fan-favorite scenes.

GOODFELLAS MONEY

In 1990, Robert De Niro complained about the feeling of fake money while filming *Goodfellas.* To appease their star, the prop master withdrew $5,000 of his own money to use in the film for the famous "counting money" scene. Once filming was complete, no one—including De Niro—was allowed to leave the set until every single dollar was accounted for and returned to the prop master.

INTERSTELLAR CORN FARM

In 2014, director Christopher Nolan was reluctant to use CGI to create the farm that played a central role in his movie *Interstellar*. Consequently, he planted 500 acres of corn on his own land to ensure that the setting looked as real as possible. He spent $100,000 to grow the corn in Western Canada, just outside of Calgary, where corn doesn't grow very well. However, the gamble paid off, resulting in a lush crop of corn that gave the film a touch of reality that would otherwise have been lost. After filming was complete, the gamble paid off even more, as Nolan had the corn harvested and sold it at a profit.

STRANGE MUSIC TRIVIA

THE "27 CLUB" OF MUSICIANS

Apparently, 27 is a bad age for musicians – numerous well-known musicians have died at that age, giving rise to the "27 Club." Some members of this undesirable club include Brian Jones, Jimi Hendrix, Janis Joplin, Jim Morrison, Kurt Cobain, and Amy Winehouse, among others. While these deaths are coincidental (and often related to drug and/or alcohol abuse and suicide), the tragic demise of young rock and rollers is a sober confirmation of the intense pressure musicians are often under in the music industry.

HIDDEN MESSAGES IN BEATLES' SONGS

Not only were the Beatles one of the most popular bands in history, but they're even more intriguing because of the speculation surrounding hidden messages and symbolism in their songs. For example, the initials of "Lucy in the Sky with Diamonds" spell LSD, which has fueled the idea that the song is about drugs. Other songs, such as "Revolution 9," "Strawberry Fields Forever," "I Am the Walrus," and "A Day in the Life," contain odd lyrics and obscure imagery that are left open to the listeners' interpretations.

The Beatles also experimented with "backmasking," or recording songs backward, accidentally recorded curse words in their songs, and hid strange phrases such as "Yawn Paul" in "I'm Only Sleeping" and "Queen says 'no' to pot-smoking FBI members" in "For You Blue."

WEIRD & WACKY WORKS OF ART

DUCHAMP'S *FOUNTAIN* URINAL

In 1917, artist Marcel Duchamp unveiled his artwork entitled *Fountain* under the pseudonym "R. Mutt." The piece, a urinal turned 90 degrees to rest on its back, was submitted to a Society of Independent Artists art show. This organization promised to accept any piece of art, as long as the artist paid the application fee. *Fountain* caused an uproar when the society did not accept it into the show, believing it was a practical joke. Duchamp, who was on the society's board, resigned in protest. Since then, the sculpture has sparked many debates on what is and isn't considered art, challenging the concept that skill needs to be involved in creating it.

CHRIS OFILI'S ELEPHANT DUNG PAINTINGS

In the late 1990s, artist Chris Ofili challenged ideas about spirituality, identity, and colonialism by creating paintings with elephant dung. His *The Holy Virgin Mary*, among other paintings, incorporated the poop with intricate designs and bright colors. The paintings were quite controversial, as many people believed he was mocking religion, and discussions about cultural appropriation, artistic freedom, and religious imagery became rampant. Despite heavy criticism, Ofili's paintings have earned praise for their originality and risk, and Ofili himself is considered one of the most influential artists in contemporary art.

CHAPTER SEVEN: SPORTS & RECREATION

ORIGINS OF POPULAR SPORTS

SOCCER

Soccer, or football, has its roots in an ancient Mesoamerican game called "tlachtli." This activity was more than just a game for the Aztecs and Mayans who played it, though; it held religious, social, and political significance, and could lead to the human sacrifice of a member from the losing team. Players could only use their hips and, in some versions, sticks to hit the ball—which was made of solid rubber and weighed as much as nine pounds—through goals or to simply keep it in play without touching the ground.

BASKETBALL

James Naismith, a physical education teacher at the International YMCA Training School in Springfield, Massachusetts, was looking for a way to keep his students active indoors during the harsh winter months. To this end, in 1891, he invented a game involving two peach baskets and a soccer ball, which combined the elements of soccer, football, and hockey. He called it "basketball," and his original thirteen rules laid the groundwork for the modern version we play today. The sport caught fire among YMCAs and schools across the United States, eventually growing into a global phenomenon.

TENNIS

In the 1100s, a game called "jeu de paume" (literally "palm game") gained popularity in France. The game was played indoors, with participants using their hands to hit a ball over a net or against a wall. It was the predecessor to the game we know today as tennis. Eventually, players began using rackets to hit the ball, and the game moved outdoors. By the 1500s, tennis had become a favorite activity among the royalty and nobility classes. The word "tennis" likely comes from the French word *tenez*, roughly translated to "hold" or—more appropriately—"receive." Players would shout this phrase to alert their opponents prior to serving the ball.

RUGBY

In 1823, legend has it that during a football (soccer) match in England, 16-year-old William Webb Ellis picked up the ball and ran with it. His fellow students thought this was ingenious and incorporated the move into their game, thus creating a new style of game known as rugby football. This sport had its own set of rules, separate from the rules for association football, but rugby didn't become an official sport until 1845 when the first written rules standardized the game. Rugby's popularity quickly spread across schools and universities in Europe before eventually finding its way around the globe.

BIZARRE SPORTS FROM AROUND THE WORLD

TOE WRESTLING

In the 1970s, four friends in Staffordshire, United Kingdom were drinking and grumbling about the dominance of American sports, none of which they could play. They decided to create a game they might be good at, and thus, toe wrestling was born. In this quirky sport, competitors go toe-to-toe (if you'll forgive the pun) and attempt to pin each other's toes for three seconds. Incredibly, the sport gained enough popularity that, in 1994, the annual World Toe Wrestling Championship debuted in Derbyshire, England—an event that, to this day, is held in a different British city each year.

BOG SNORKELING

This odd sport started as a fundraising event in Wales in 1976. However, it became so popular that it evolved into an annual championship, with competitors donning snorkels and flippers to swim through a water-filled trench in a peat bog. They must navigate murky waters filled with peat, vegetation, and mud to complete the course as quickly as possible without using traditional swimming strokes—only their flippers! The championship attracts participants from all over the world, from serious athletes to people just looking for a bit of camaraderie and competition.

EXTREME IRONING

Yet another English creation, Extreme Ironing debuted in 1997 but has since gained an international following. This humorous sport combines mundane ironing with the blood-pumping thrill of extreme outdoor activities. Participants take their equipment to daring locations—forests, mountains, even underwater—ironing while rock climbing, skiing, diving, or skydiving. While this activity definitely pushes the boundaries of what is considered a sport, part of the fun is seeing who can come up with the wildest approach to performing this normally mundane domestic chore.

BOSSABALL

For those who can't make up their mind about which sport they want to play, there's Bossaball! This sport originated in Spain in 2004, combining elements of volleyball, soccer, gymnastics, and the Brazilian martial art of capoeira. Played on an inflatable court equipped with trampolines on each side of a net, Bossaball calls for two teams of four to six players each to use their hands, feet, and heads to pass a ball over the net. If the ball lands on the opponent's side, the team scores a point. Players need to be quite acrobatic to excel at this sport, but it's quickly gaining a devout following for the "bossa" (translated as "style, flair or attitude" in Indian Spanish) participants display.

FERRET LEGGING

The absurd sport of Ferret Legging is yet another wonderful contribution from England. The first known Ferret Legging competition was held in the 1970s, and while the sport is quite entertaining for spectators, it's more of a test of endurance for participants. Competitors tie their pants at the ankles and insert ferrets into their pants to see who can last the longest without allowing the ferrets to escape or suffer serious injury. Understandably, bites and scratches are common in this sport, and competitions have become a true test of pain tolerance and bravery.

CHEESE-ROLLING

England is definitely the king of bizarre sports, with another entry from Gloucestershire. Cheese-rolling dates back to the 1800s and involves rolling and chasing a 7-9-pound wheel of cheese down a steep hill. The goal is to be the first person to get both themselves and their wheel of cheese across the finish line at the bottom of the hill. Participants hurl their bodies after their cheese, risking serious injury and massive embarrassment. These Cheese-rolling events are heavily attended, attracting locals and visitors from all over the world.

OCTOPUSH

Also referred to as underwater hockey, Octopush has its roots in—you guessed it—England, dating back to the 1950s. Players equip themselves with snorkels, masks, fins, and short sticks (called "pushers") and jump into a swimming pool. Once underwater, they attempt to push a puck into the opposing team's goal. Combining elements of hockey, snorkeling, and swimming, the sport requires teamwork, concentration, strategy, and breath control. Octopush is popular worldwide, with organized leagues in the United Kingdom, Japan, and South Africa, among others.

STRANGE SPORTS RECORDS

- In 2010, Wim Hof, also known as "The Iceman," for obvious reasons, spent 44 minutes in direct, full-body contact with ice, though the resulting record has since been broken. He also set records for the fastest half-marathon run while barefoot on ice or snow and the farthest swim under ice.

- In 2008, Ashrita Furman crushed 80 raw eggs with his head in one minute, setting a new Guinness World Record. Ashrita actually holds several egg-related records and has set over 600 records in his lifetime!
- In Belgium, Jimmy De Frenne broke the record for the longest time sitting on a toilet when he spent 116 hours on one in 2019.
- Don Gorske entered the Guinness Book of World Records in 2018 for eating more than 28,000 Big Mac burgers between 1972 and 2018.
- In 2011, Andrew Lawrence ran and completed the London Marathon dressed as a banana in two hours and 47 minutes, marking the fastest time anyone has run a marathon dressed as a fruit.
- In 2019, Ted Hastings broke the record for most T-shirts worn at once when he put on 260 shirts, ranging from medium to 20X in size.
- Antony Edwards of the UK holds the record for riding the fastest lawnmower in history, topping out at a speed of 143.193 miles per hour in 2021.
- Ten-year-old Sophie Smith charmed 567 worms to the surface at Britain's World Worm Charming Championship on June 27, 2009, a record that still stands today.
- On August 27, 2014, Dries Feremans of Belgium set the record for the furthest distance that a mobile phone has been thrown when he threw his phone 362 feet, three inches—roughly the length of a football field!
- Brian "Young Gun" Krause of the United States holds the world record for the longest cherry pit spit in a competition at 93 feet, 6.5 inches, a record he set in 2004.
- In 2008, Huy Giang set the record for the most rotations from a hanging power drill in one minute by making 148 revolutions.

- The aptly named Dolphin Ratheesh from India set a world record for the farthest swim while wearing handcuffs and leg irons when he swam 6.21 miles in 2020.
- Bernie Boehm holds the world record for the longest time spinning a basketball on a guitar. His basketball spun for 32.46 in 2021.
- In 2015, Japan's Kenichi Ito set a world record for the fastest 100-meter run on all fours, running it in 15.71 seconds.
- Christian Roberto Lopez Rodriguez ran 100 meters wearing swim fins in 10.69 seconds and set the record in 2024—which means it's faster to run with swim fins than it is to run on all fours! Rodrigez also holds the record for the fastest 100 meters while wearing stiletto high heels, with a time of 12.82 seconds.
- Samuel Groth holds the record for the fastest tennis serve ever recorded at 163.7 miles per hour.
- Some people can solve puzzle cubes, and others can skateboard, but not many people can do both at the same time. However, British skateboarder George Scholey set the world record for most puzzle cubes solved on a skateboard in 2022—500 cubes in 40 minutes!

SPORTS-RELATED FUN FACTS

- Olympic gold medals are made mostly of silver and plated with a thin layer of gold.
- The longest tennis match in Wimbledon history took place in 2010, with players John Isner and Nicholas Mahut playing an 11-hour, five-minute match over three days.
- The Stanley Cup, which is awarded annually to the best hockey team in the National Hockey League, can hold the contents of up to fourteen cans of beer.
- Instead of gold medals, ancient Olympic winners received a crown of olive branches.

- Despite being one of the most famous Major League baseball players of all time, Babe Ruth only received one Most Valuable Player award during his career.
- The largest soccer (football) stadium in the world is the Rungrado 1st of May Stadium in Pyongyang, North Korea. It can seat 150,000 spectators!
- In the first official basketball game played on December 21, 1891, the final score was 1-0, with William R. Chase scoring the only basket for the winning team.

CHAPTER EIGHT: MIND & BODY

MENTAL HEALTH TIPS & TRICKS

MINDFULNESS & MEDITATION

To reduce stress, anxiety, and depression, help regulate emotions, promote greater resilience, and foster a sense of inner peace, practice mindfulness and meditation. These centering activities that focus on present-moment awareness can also provide physical benefits such as lower blood pressure, boosted immunity, and reduced inflammation. Focus on your breathing, inhaling and exhaling slowly and deeply to empty your mind of anything except the here and now. Practicing for a few minutes each day to develop this skill can greatly improve your quality of life and overall happiness.

IMPORTANCE OF SLEEP

As you've probably been told many times throughout your life, sleep is crucial for your overall health and well-being. It's not just about feeling rested and ready to take on a new day—it's also about allowing your body time to repair and recover from everything you put it through when you're awake! As you sleep, your brain consolidates your memories and processes information, while your body shores up its immune system, which helps you fight off illnesses and infections. When you don't get enough sleep, you could become irritable, have trouble focusing, and even increase your risk of developing chronic conditions like diabetes and heart disease.

EXERCISE & MENTAL WELL-BEING

As with sleep, you already know it's important to get enough exercise, but do you know why? When you exercise, your body releases endorphins, neurotransmitters that reduce pain and boost mood. There's a reason you feel happier after you work out, and it's not just because your workout is over for the day! Regular exercise can alleviate symptoms of anxiety and depression, promoting feelings of relaxation and contentment. Plus, you'll also sleep better—physical activity tires your body out, preparing it for rest. You don't have to hit the gym hard to get these benefits, though; even a brisk walk can do wonders for your mental state.

JOURNALING FOR STRESS RELIEF

Keeping a written journal is a powerful way to relieve stress, as it allows you to express yourself freely, without fear of judgment. When you write down your thoughts, experiences, and feelings, you'll gain clarity and perspective on situations that might be troubling you. Writing helps you process emotions, identify triggers, and discover solutions to challenges. Let go of negative thoughts by getting them out of your head and into your journal, allowing you to move forward with a clear mind.

STRANGE BODY FACTS

HUMANS GLOW IN THE DARK

While humans don't actually glow like fireflies, research suggests that we emit a faint light, though it's not bright enough to see with the naked eye. This phenomenon, called "bioluminescence," is thought to be caused by chemical reactions inside our bodies. These involve molecules like reactive oxygen species (ROS) and adenosine triphosphate, but the actual process is not yet completely understood. So, even though we don't light up like glow sticks, we all have a bit of light inside us—and that's pretty cool.

YOUR "SCENT"SITIVE NOSE

The human nose can detect over one trillion different scents, making it one of the most sensitive scent detectors in the animal kingdom. We are particularly sensitive to scents associated with survival and reproduction, so we're most likely to smell food, spoiled or rancid odors, smoke, and pheromones before we detect odors like inert gasses and artificial scents. However, as remarkable as our nose is, it pales in comparison to a dog's nose, which has 300 million scent receptors, compared to our measly six million.

BONE IS STRONGER THAN STEEL

Even though broken bones seem to indicate that human skeletons are fragile, they're actually incredibly strong. Pound for pound, bone is stronger than steel, due to its composition. Bones consist of a complex maze of collagen fibers reinforced with calcium and other minerals. This combination makes bones flexible yet resilient, so they can withstand significant pressure without breaking. On the other hand, steel is rigid and will break under stress. Moreover, bone is constantly repairing micro-damages that occur under everyday use, making them stronger by the day!

THE BODY'S NATURAL PAINKILLERS

Your body is equipped with natural painkillers, produced by your brain under specific circumstances, such as when you laugh, exercise, or even eat spicy food. These painkillers, called "endorphins," bind to the same receptors as pain medications to effectively block pain signals. They also produce euphoria and feelings of well-being, helping you naturally cope with discomfort and stress. Endorphins can also boost your immune system and reduce inflammation, both of which are important for long-term health. Other activities that trigger endorphin production include listening to music, meditation, socializing, getting a massage, hugging, and—of course—eating chocolate.

WEIRD BRAIN TEASERS & PUZZLES

THE MONTY HALL PROBLEM

Named after Monty Hall, the host of the game show *Let's Make a Deal,* the Monty Hall problem is a famous probability puzzle that has confounded people for decades. In the scenario, contestants choose one of three doors. Behind two doors are goats, and behind one door is a prize. After the contestant selects a door, the host, who knows what's behind each door, opens one of the remaining doors to reveal a goat. The contestant can then switch their choice to the other unopened door or stay with their original choice. Interestingly, based on statistics, switching actually gives them a better chance of winning the prize!

THE STROOP EFFECT

This interesting phenomenon highlights the brain's challenges in overriding automatic processes such as reading. In the experiment, participants are shown color names written in mismatched ink. For example, the word "Red" might be written in blue ink. The participants are asked to name the ink color while ignoring the word's meaning. However, because of the automatic process of reading, participants usually struggle, naming the word they read instead of the ink's actual color. The exercise reveals insights into attention, cognitive control, and language processing.

"TWO DOORS, ONE GUARD ALWAYS LIES"

In this puzzle, made famous by the movie *Labyrinth*, you face two doors, one leading to safety and the other to danger. Each door is protected by a guard, one of whom always tells the truth, while the other always lies. To determine which door leads to safety, you are only allowed to ask one question. The key is to ask, "If I asked the other guard which door leads to safety, what would they say?" No matter which guard you ask, the answer to this question is always the same: The truth-teller points to the wrong door—because that's what the lying guard would say—and the lying guard points to the same door—because they're lying. You would choose the opposite door to reach safety.

VISUAL ILLUSIONS

Visual illusions like the Necker Cube, Muller-Lyer, and Ames room trick your brain into seeing things that aren't really there.

The Necker Cube is a basic line drawing of a cube that flips between two perspectives. Your brain can't decide which face is the front, causing it to switch back and forth. The Muller-Lyer illusion involves two lines of equal length with arrows at each end. One line appears longer because of the arrows' orientation. The Ames room illusion creates a distorted room that appears normal if you view it from a certain angle. People inside the room will appear to grow or shrink depending on your angle because the room's true shape is hidden.

MIND-BOGGLING PSYCHOLOGICAL PHENOMENA

THE MANDELA EFFECT

Have you ever disagreed with someone about an event in your past that you both attended or learned about at the same time? You may have experienced the Mandela Effect. This phenomenon is named after Nelson Mandela, who many people falsely remember dying in prison in the 1980s even though he didn't actually die until 2013. The effect suggests that collective false memories can spring into being because of misinformation, social influence, and the brain's tendency to fill in gaps. It highlights the fallibility of human memory and how easily it can be influenced.

DEJÀ VU

Have you ever had the eerie feeling that you've already been through a current situation, even though it's happening for the first time? This is called *dejà vu,* from the French "already seen." This sensation occurs when your brain processes a new experience by comparing it to an experience in your past that makes it feel familiar. Scientists don't fully understand this phenomenon, but believe it relates to a mix-up between your short-term and long-term memory pathways; it also has links to auras caused by seizures and migraines, but don't worry—just because you get déjà vu doesn't mean there's anything wrong with your brain! The feeling usually doesn't last long, but it can be disconcerting, causing you to wonder how the mind works.

THE PLACEBO EFFECT

When you were young and suffered a minor injury like a scrape or bruise, your mother might have kissed it to make it feel better. Of course, her kiss didn't have the power to make your injury disappear, but you probably felt better anyway. This is called the "placebo effect," a phenomenon that causes people to experience improvements in health or symptoms after receiving a treatment that has no actual therapeutic value. For example, they might have received a sugar pill instead of actual medicine, but since the person believes it will work, the brain releases chemicals that effectively alleviate symptoms or improve a condition. Placebos are often used in clinical trials to test the effectiveness of new drugs.

COGNITIVE DISSONANCE

This uncomfortable phenomenon occurs when you hold two contradicting beliefs or behaviors. For example, if you value health but smoke cigarettes, the conflict between your actions and beliefs creates mental tension. When this occurs, we tend to want to reduce the tension by changing our behavior (quitting smoking), justifying our behavior (saying, "I only smoke when I drink alcohol"), or downplaying the conflict (saying, "Smoking relieves my stress"). The term was coined in 1957 to explain why we often rationalize or alter our attitudes to align with our actions to gain internal peace.

CHAPTER NINE: TRAVEL & GEOGRAPHY

STRANGE TRAVEL DESTINATIONS

THE CATACOMBS OF PARIS

Originally constructed as limestone quarries, this unique travel destination exists beneath the streets of Paris, France. This eerie underground vault contains the mortal remains of more than six million people! These remains were transferred to the Catacombs in the 18th century when above-ground cemeteries became too crowded. Visitors can explore a small section of the tomb to view tunnels lined with skulls and bones. As if that wasn't creepy enough, the dimly lit passages and cave-like atmosphere create an unforgettable—if unsettling—experience that serves as a haunting reminder of the city's history.

THE DOOR TO HELL

Also known as the Darvaza gas crater, the Door to Hell in Turkmenistan is a huge pit that has burned continuously for about 50 years! Though its origins are still debated, some believe that Soviet engineers accidentally created the pit while drilling for natural gas in 1971. Others have suggested that it formed naturally in the 1960s and was set on fire by geologists in the 1980s in an effort to prevent the spread of methane gas; however, they underestimated just how much gas it contained, expecting it to burn out in a few days. Instead, the pit, which is about 230 feet wide and 98 feet deep, has become a hot spot for tourists intrigued by the mesmerizing sight of glowing flames and intense heat.

THE ISLAND OF DOLLS

The Island of the Dolls, A UNESCO World Heritage Site, is located near Mexico City in the Xochimilco canals. The island is covered with thousands of dolls, hanging from trees and structures. Legend has it that in the 1950s, the reclusive owner of the island, Don Julian Santana Barrera, found a young girl who'd drowned in the canal; Barrera claimed that after she died, he found a doll drifting down the canal. He hung the doll up as an offering to her spirit and spent nearly 50 years collecting other dolls to create the terrifying scene on the island today. Visitors attracted to the macabre spectacle have reported hearing the dolls whispering to each other, opening their arms and eyes, and moving their heads, making this a prime destination for dark tourism.

THE CROOKED FOREST

Located near the Polish village of Gryfino, the Crooked Forest is home to approximately 400 pine trees that curve to the north nearly 90 degrees at the base before turning upright. The trees were planted in the 1930s, but to this day, no one fully understands what caused them to grow in this strange shape. Some experts suggest human intervention caused the unnatural bend in the trees, perhaps to supply tinder for wooden cartwheels or boat building, while others believe they grew naturally due to environmental factors. Regardless of the "why," the spot has become a popular place for photography, given its unique features.

UNUSUAL GEOGRAPHICAL FEATURES

SALAR DE UYUNI

The world's largest salt flats, spanning over 4,000 square miles, are in southwest Bolivia. The flats were formed by the evaporation of prehistoric lakes, now covered with a thick crust of salt stretching as far as the eye can see. During the rainy season, a thin layer of water covers the salt, transforming the flats and turning the landscape into an otherworldly reflection of the sky. It's an ideal location for unique photography sessions, but all visitors enjoy the incredible optical illusions that crop up across the flats.

THE GIANT'S CAUSEWAY

Along the Antrim coast in Northern Ireland is the Giant's Causeway, the remnants of an ancient volcanic eruption that formed over 40,000 interlocking, mostly hexagonal basalt columns. While the columns were formed naturally, an Irish legend says the giant Finn McCool built the causeway of steppingstones to cross the sea to Scotland. The causeway is a UNESCO World Heritage Site and a dramatic attraction not to be missed.

MOUNT RORAIMA

This flat-topped mountain, known as a tepui, rises 9,200 feet above the surrounding rainforest at the border of Venezuela, Brazil, and Guyana. Its summit is often covered in mist, lending it an otherworldly appearance. In fact, Mount Roraima has been the inspiration for numerous legends and stories, including Arthur Conan Doyle's *The Lost World*. Its unique location has made it home to rare plants and animals found nowhere else in the world, such as the Roraima bush toad, certain orchid species, and carnivorous pitcher plants.

BLOOD FALLS

In the McMurdo Dry Valleys in Antarctica, an unusual phenomenon causes red water to seep from the nearby Taylor Glacier. The striking crimson water coalesces into a waterfall that spills onto the white ice, creating a dramatic contrast in colors. The red color comes from the iron-rich saltwater trapped beneath the glacier. When iron comes into contact with air, it oxidizes, turning red in a process similar to that which forms rust. Iron-rich water is also home to ancient microbes that grow in the absence of sunlight and oxygen, making Blood Falls an intriguing extreme ecosystem for scientists to study.

WEIRD TRAVEL CUSTOMS & TRADITIONS

FINGER-CUTTING OF THE DANI TRIBE

For hundreds of years, the Dani Tribe—particularly its women—in Indonesia has practiced the intense tradition of finger-cutting in marriage ceremonies and to express grief when a close family member dies. Female tribe members may amputate a part of one of their fingers during mourning rituals. The bloodletting symbolizes and physically manifests the pain and loss they feel inside from the death of their loved one. In the Dani language, the ritual is called *Ikipalin* and comes from their deep cultural belief in the connection between the physical and spiritual worlds. Today, finger-cutting is discouraged by local authorities but is still practiced at times within the tribe.

BABY JUMPING FESTIVAL

El Colacho, or the Baby Jumping Festival, occurs annually in Castrillo de Murcia, Spain, during the feast of Corpus Christi in May. The festival features men dressed as devils who jump over babies lying on mattresses in the street. The festival and ritual date back to the 1600s and are thought to cleanse the babies of original sin and keep them safe from evil spirits and disease. Visitors find the sight of costumed men leaping over rows of babies both shocking and fascinating, but the festival is a cherished cultural event for locals that's highly anticipated each year.

MONKEY BUFFET FESTIVAL

In a gesture of gratitude toward monkeys, residents of Lopburi, Thailand, hold their annual Monkey Buffet Festival, in which the hosts present tables covered in fruits, vegetables, and other treats for macaque monkeys to feast on. The festival began in 1989 when hotelier Yongyuth Kitwattananusont wanted to thank the long-tailed macaques for bringing tourists to Lopburi. Tourism is the main source of income for locals, who are said to descend from the monkey-headed Hindu god Hanuman. The festival takes place in the ruins of the Phra Prang Sam Yot temple and features mostly bananas, apples, pineapples, and watermelon.

OBSCURE COUNTRY FACTS

ETHIOPIA USES A DIFFERENT CALENDAR

The Ethiopian calendar, known as the Ge'ez calendar, is based on the ancient Egyptian Coptic calendar. It consists of thirteen months, 12 of which have 30 days, and one has five or six days in leap years. This 13th month is called "Pagume" and is designed to align with the solar cycle. The word Pagume comes from the Greek word *epagomene*, which translates to "days forgotten when a year is calculated." This calendar is based on Christ's date of annunciation, so the current year in Ethiopia is usually seven or eight years behind the Gregorian calendar that most other countries use.

LIECHTENSTEIN CAN BE RENTED FOR EVENTS

Since 2010, Lichtenstein, a small European country, has offered an interesting opportunity that allows the entire country to be rented out for private events, such as weddings, corporate events, or big parties. Since renting out Liechtenstein is extremely expensive—starting at $70,000 per night—reserving it is a luxury reserved for the wealthy. Renting out the country provides exclusive access to accommodations and landmarks, and the government will even personalize its street signs to further customize the experience, which is considered the height of privacy and luxury.

THE WORLD'S OLDEST REPUBLIC

Established in AD 301, San Marino, a small country located within Italy, is the world's oldest continuous republic, having retained its independence and republican government for over 1,700 years. It was the first country to recognize and commit to democratic principles and self-governance and is still considered an example for other countries to follow. In 1861, most of the Italian peninsula was unified into a single country, but San Marino remains steadfastly independent, the fifth-smallest country in the world.

GROSS NATIONAL HAPPINESS

Bhutan, a landlocked country located in south-central Asia, broke new ground in measuring the progress of its citizens in 2008 when it carried out a national survey to measure happiness with empirical data. The government sent out the Gross National Happiness Survey asking its population questions about health, education, community, and environmental issues to help form policies prioritizing happiness over economic growth. The survey represented the first time that a government attempted to redefine national prosperity beyond material wealth. The government repeated the survey in 2010, 2015, and again in 2022, with the percentage of people considering themselves deeply or extremely happy improving each time.

CHAPTER TEN: TECHNOLOGY

INNOVATIONS IN BATHROOM TECHNOLOGY

SMART TOILETS WITH BIDET FEATURES

While the bidet itself originated in France, the first smart toilet, the "Washlet," actually appeared in Japan in the 1980s. Originally, they only had basic bidet attachments, so the real innovation is in the "smart" toilets that offer bidet features, along with amenities such as heated seats, air drying capabilities, and adjustable water temperature. These toilets incorporate sensors for automatic flushing, built-in air purifiers, and even deodorizers. They're designed not only to promote hygiene, but also provide comfort, convenience, and conservation, as they reduce the need for toilet paper.

WATER-SAVING DUAL FLUSH TOILETS

Dual flush toilets debuted in Australia in the 1980s to address drought concerns, though designs had been developed previously in Japan and America. They've since gained global popularity for their environmental benefits. These toilets have two flush options: one that uses less water for tinkles and another that uses more water for those "solid" trips to the restroom. Typically, the small flush expends 1.2 gallons of water, compared to the 1.6 gallons used for the larger flush. The toilets' design encourages water conservation without much effort on the part of the user, making them smart and environmentally friendly options for both homes and businesses.

MOTION SENSOR FAUCETS & SOAP DISPENSERS

In the late 20th century, hands-free faucets and soap dispensers began to appear in public restrooms, kitchens, and hospitals. These faucets and soap dispensers rely on sensors to detect hand movement, which triggers water flow or the release of soap without the user touching their surfaces. They were initially developed to accommodate those with arthritis and reduce water waste, but when the COVID-19 pandemic hit in 2020, they became standard to avoid transmission of the virus from contaminated surfaces. Since then, hands-free faucets and soap dispensers have found their way into homes to minimize the spread of germs.

SELF-CLEANING TOILET BOWLS

With origins dating back to 1907 with the introduction of vortex-flushing toilets, self-cleaning toilet bowls have made an undesirable chore much easier. These toilets use special coatings, electrolyzed water, or ultraviolet light to kill bacteria and break down stains on the porcelain. The result is less manual scrubbing and more time for other, more enjoyable tasks. The technology used in these bowls has continued to evolve, with the addition of sensors and timers for regular cleaning cycles. These innovations have improved convenience and sanitation in homes, businesses, and public facilities. As the price for this luxury falls, expect it to become standard in even more places.

WEIRD GADGETS & GIZMOS

TOILET PAPER DISPENSING ROBOTS

Similar to hands-free faucets and soap dispensers, toilet paper dispensing robots were invented in the early 2000s to address hygiene concerns and make restroom management more efficient. The robots use sensors to detect when someone has used the toilet so they can dispense a controlled amount of toilet paper. This prevents overuse and ensures enough toilet paper is available in high-traffic areas. The more modern toilet paper dispensing robots are equipped with automatic refilling features and maintenance alerts, so they basically run themselves!

BLUETOOTH-ENABLED TOILET SEATS

The smartest of smart toilets these days come equipped with Bluetooth-enabled toilet seats that allow users to control features like bidet functions and heated seats. Some even allow users to play music from their phones or other devices! Bluetooth connectivity enables users to customize their settings, use remote control to operate the toilet, and improve their comfort and hygiene. Initially, only the wealthy could afford this technology, but Bluetooth-enabled toilet seats are gaining mainstream popularity as luxurious bathrooms become a highly desired amenity among average homeowners, particularly those who want to create a spa-like experience in their own homes.

TOILET NIGHT LIGHTS WITH MOTION SENSORS

Why did toilet night lights with motion sensors take until the mid-2010s to become available? It's a mystery, as anyone who has ever stumbled to the toilet at night can tell you! These miracle devices illuminate the toilet bowl when their sensors detect motion in the dark, allowing you to use the toilet easily without turning on the overhead light. These lights come in a variety of colors and brightness levels that can be adjusted to suit your specific needs. Luxury hotels have begun incorporating these lights to improve guest safety as they attempt to navigate unfamiliar spaces at night.

NO-TOUCH TOILETS

As with hands-free faucets and soap dispensers, the inventors of no-touch toilets were inspired by the desire to reduce germ transmission in public and commercial bathrooms. In some models, the toilet seat will even rise for male users as they face the toilet, preventing any little "surprises" the next time someone has to take a seat! When the user moves away, the toilet automatically flushes, saving you from having to touch the flusher and reducing the spread of germs. These toilets are extremely popular in public places like airports, but they are beginning to show up in private residences as well.

FUN FACTS ABOUT THE HISTORY OF TOILET TECH

THE FIRST TOILET PAPER

Historical evidence suggests that the first toilet paper was produced in China in the 6th century. At first, only members of the imperial family used the soft sheets made from mulberry bark and other fibrous materials, finely processed for absorbency and comfort. Since only royals and dignitaries used this paper, it was associated with luxury, though it greatly improved hygiene as well. Eventually, production techniques improved, allowing toilet paper to be produced in higher quantities, which led to usage across classes, and the rest, as they say, is history!

THE FIRST FLUSH TOILET

Initially known as the "Ajax," the first flush toilet appeared in 1596, the brainchild of Sir John Harington. An amateur poet whose risqué writings caused his exile from Queen Elizabeth I's court, Harington designed a toilet with a system of handles, levers, and weights to let in water from a connected cistern. The water would flush the waste into an underground cesspool, and a valve under the toilet seat controlled the flow of water, allowing for periodic flushing. Harington's goal was to reduce waste accumulation indoors, and while his design was not well received at the time, it laid the foundation for modern flush toilets.

THE FIRST PATENT FOR A FLUSHING TOILET

Speaking of flush toilets, Alexander Cumming received the first patent for a flushing toilet in 1775, marking a major milestone in sanitation history. His design improved the flushing mechanism and included an S-bend, which prevented sewer gases from rising into buildings—solving the issue of lingering odors that Harington's design had left behind. S-bends are still in use in modern toilets, proving that sometimes, the simplest solution can revolutionize technology for the ages! Cumming's invention and patent came about as society began to recognize sanitation as a public health concern that required appropriate attention and practical, innovative solutions.

THE POPULARIZATION OF THE FLUSH TOILET

Returning to Thomas Crapper, who is often mistaken for inventing the flush toilet, we now look a little deeper at his actual contributions. Crapper was a plumber and a businessman born in the 1800s whose improvements in the flush toilet and marketing genius popularized the appliance throughout England. In fact, he gained a Royal Warrant from King Edward VII for his high-quality toilets, leading to Crapper's name becoming synonymous with the porcelain sanitation device. In particular, Crapper's ballcock mechanism for efficient water control and the U-bend, an improvement on the S-bend, continue to impact modern toilet design even today.

QUIRKY TECH-RELATED TRIVIA

THE FIRST WEBCAM

In 1991, scientists at the University of Cambridge in a remote office were annoyed by having to leave their desks to see if the coffee was finished brewing—often, they found themselves disappointed when they made the trip to get a hot cup of java. Consequently, these brilliant minds created the first webcam, the "Trojan Room coffee pot," which allowed them to monitor the pot remotely. The camera captured images of the coffee pot every few seconds, transmitting them over the network so that anyone with access could see when the coffee was ready. The camera was connected to the fledgling World Wide Web a few years later, gaining international fame until its retirement in 2001.

THE FIRST MOBILE PHONE CALL

While cell phones didn't become mainstream until the 21st century, the first mobile phone call was actually made in 1973. Martin Cooper, a researcher with Motorola, stood on a New York City sidewalk and placed a call to Joel Engel, a rival researcher at Bell Labs. The phone, a DynaTAC weighing nearly 2.5 pounds, represented a major breakthrough in mobile technology and laid the groundwork for developing smaller and more efficient mobile phones. This achievement marked the beginning of the cell phone revolution that continues to this day.

THE QWERTY KEYBOARD LAYOUT

In the 1870s, newspaper publisher and Wisconsin politician Christopher Latham Sholes designed the QWERTY keyboard layout to prevent jamming in early typewriters. Sholes' keyboard spread the most commonly used letters to make sure typists could perform their work without the mechanical issues that had plagued them until then. Though more efficient keyboard layouts have since appeared, none have gained the popularity of the QWERTY layout—mostly because major typewriter manufacturers adopted it, making it the standard keyboard in English-speaking countries.

THE FIRST COMPUTER WORM

Bob Thomas, a programmer at BBN Technologies, created the first computer virus in the early 1970s. He named it "Creeper," designed as an experimental self-replicating program to test the security of ARPANET, the precursor to today's Internet. The virus would replicate itself and move from computer to computer, displaying the message: "I'M THE CREEPER; CATCH ME IF YOU CAN!" Creeper wasn't a malicious virus, but it demonstrated the potential for software to spread autonomously over a network. Another BBN engineer, Ray Tomlinson, then developed the "Reaper" program to eradicate Creeper, making it the first antivirus software.

THE FIRST EMAIL SYSTEM

MAILBOX, the first email system, debuted in 1965 as part of the Massachusetts Institute of Technology's Compatible Time-Sharing System (CTSS) project. MAILBOX allowed users to leave messages for each other on a central computer that could be accessed remotely through the ARPANET network. Users could compose their messages offline and send them once they are connected to the network. This revolutionary system laid the foundation for modern email communication, including concepts like the inbox, outbox, and message storage. Since the World Wide Web wasn't created until 1991, email is actually older than the Internet!

THE FIRST PALM-SIZED COMPUTER

These days, we basically have an entire computer on our phones, but the first palm-sized computer, the Atari Portfolio, was introduced in 1989. It featured a compact design that resembled a notebook, powered by AA batteries, offering users basic productivity tools like a text editor and spreadsheet software, but expansion cards also allowed them to play games on its monochrome LCD screen. Two years later, a young John Connor used the Atari Portfolio in Terminator 2 to hack into an ATM, gaining the key to the Cyberdyne lab vault.

PAC-MAN: AN EARLY FORM OF AI

The ethics of Artificial Intelligence (AI) are wildly debated today, but an early form of AI was used in the Namco smash-hit video game Pac-Man. Inky, Pinky, Blinky, and Clyde, the four ghosts that chase Pac-Man around the screen, each have a distinct personality, with different methods for trying to catch Pac-Man: Inky and Pinky usually attempt to corner him, Blinky chases him directly, and Clyde alternatively gives chase and runs away. As the game progresses, the ghosts' speed and behavior change, creating an innovative challenge that fascinated players at the time. In fact, there are a multitude of online articles analyzing the particular traits of each ghost's AI if you want to learn more!

CHAPTER ELEVEN: MYTHOLOGY & FOLKLORE

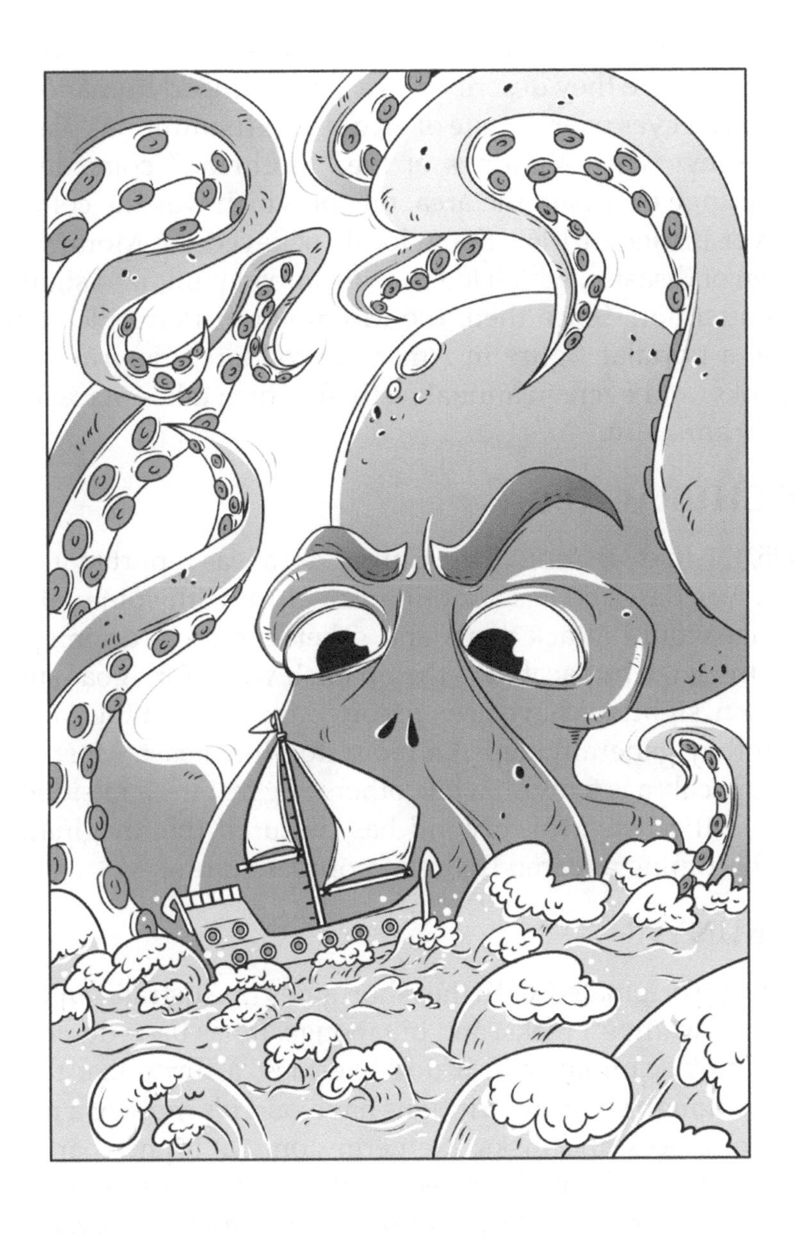

STRANGE CRYPTIDS FROM AROUND THE WORLD

THE MOTHMAN OF POINT PLEASANT

In 1966, two residents of Point Pleasant, West Virginia, reported seeing a creature they described as a large, winged humanoid with glowing red eyes near the site of an old WWII munitions plant. The legend grew when sightings of the "Mothman" coincided with other strange events in the area, one of which was the collapse of the Silver Bridge in 1967. Some locals believed the Mothman was an omen of disaster, which led to widespread panic and significant media attention. Since then, the Mothman of Point Pleasant has become a popular figure in American folklore, inspiring movies and books, and even an annual festival, which takes place in Point Pleasant annually.

THE CHUPACABRA

In 1995, the first sighting of the Chupacabra was reported in Puerto Rico. It was described as a reptilian creature with spines along its back that would attack goats and other livestock, draining their blood. In fact, Chupacabra is the Spanish word for "goat-sucker." Since then, sightings have been reported throughout the Americas, though they generally depict a more dog-like beast. Most believe the Chupacabra is a myth, while others suggest it's a misidentified animal. Either way, this cryptid has captured the imagination of many, becoming a feared figure in popular culture.

THE BUNYIP

The Bunyip originated with the Aborigines in Australia and is said to inhabit swamps, creeks, and billabongs. It has been described as a large, furry animal with a dog-like face, a horse-like tail, and flippers, though some descriptions have said it's more of a monster with a long neck and tusks. It emerges only at night, roaring and frightening people with its eerie appearance. Rumors of this mythical creature have been around for centuries and, even today, often serve as a cautionary tale to keep kids away from dangerous waters.

THE KAPPA

Often described as a green humanoid with a turtle-like body, beak, and webbed hands and feet, the Kappa is a mythical creature in Japanese folklore inhabiting rivers and ponds. This creature has a distinct water-filled divot on its head, which is the source of its power. It's depicted as a mischievous, often malevolent being known to pull people into water. However, sometimes, the Kappa can be polite and even defeated if you can get it to bow and spill the water from its head. Oddly enough, Kappa are also said to enjoy cucumbers and sumo wrestling!

THE KRAKEN

A mainstay in Norse mythology, the Kraken is a gigantic, tentacled creature said to be so huge that it could be mistaken for an island! According to legend, the Kraken lurks off the coasts of Norway, Iceland, and Greenland, terrorizing fishermen and sailors. When it surfaces, it can create massive whirlpools that drag ships down to the depths of the ocean. Most likely, these stories were inspired by giant squid sightings, as males can grow up to 33 feet long, while females can surpass that, growing up to 43 feet long.

THE BANSHEE

In Irish mythology, the Banshee is a supernatural being characterized by an eerie wail. In most stories, the Banshee is depicted as a pale, gaunt female spirit with long, flowing hair and red eyes from constant crying. The Banshee's mournful keening is believed to precede news of the death of a family member, and she can often be seen washing bloodstained clothing or combing her hair near rivers, lakes, and ponds. She isn't considered dangerous, merely a harbinger to warn loved ones of an approaching tragedy.

THE JERSEY DEVIL

In the Pine Barrens of New Jersey, USA, the Jersey Devil is said to lurk. This mythical creature is described as having a kangaroo-like body with a horse or goat's head. It also features leathery bat-like wings, small arms with clawed fingers, horns, cloven hooves, and a forked tail. Legend has it that the Jersey Devil was born in 1735 to a frustrated woman—Mother Leeds—who cursed her 13th child, resulting in the monstrous creature. Known for the mysterious footprints left in its wake and eerie screeches, the Jersey Devil has been reportedly sighted in the area for more than 250 years.

THE WENDIGO

In the Algonquian culture of North America, the Wendigo is described as a malevolent spirit or monster that lives in cold, northern forests. It's described as a skeletal creature with sunken eyes, ash-gray skin, and an insatiable hunger for human flesh. Legend has it that the Wendigo is born to cannibalistic humans, resulting in a monstrous creature that preys on humans, growing with every person it consumes. It symbolizes gluttony, winter, famine, and isolation, sometimes even said to possess humans overwhelmed with greed.

MYTHOLOGICAL ORIGINS OF COMMON BELIEFS

THE TOOTH FAIRY

The tradition of the Tooth Fairy dates back to medieval European folklore, in which children's teeth were burned or buried to spare them from suffering in the afterlife or to keep witches from using them in their spells. However, the story transformed as it spread across the globe. For example, in Norse mythology, the Tooth Fairy took children's teeth, giving them to warriors as good luck charms, while in France, parts of Scotland, and elsewhere, the fairy takes the form of a little mouse instead. In America, the modern Tooth

Fairy concept was first recorded in the early 20th century, where it combined the European tradition of tooth collecting with the idea of leaving a small reward in exchange. By the 1920s, the Tooth Fairy had cemented its place in American culture as a magical figure that leaves a reward in exchange for lost baby teeth.

FRIDAY THE 13TH

The superstition surrounding Friday the 13th is likely due to the negative associations surrounding both Fridays and the number 13. In many cultures, Friday has long been considered an unlucky day associated with tragedy and misfortune, notably the Christian belief that Christ was crucified on a Friday, along with the British tradition of hanging criminals at the end of the week. The number 13 is also considered unlucky in many cultures: In Norse mythology, the trickster god Loki joined a dinner party as its 13th guest, ultimately deceiving the blind god Hodr into killing Balder, god of light and joy, while the Last Supper of Christian faith also had 13 attendees. Because of these various traditions, when the number 13 is combined with a Friday, it's thought to be doubly unlucky—a day to avoid risks.

KNOCKING ON WOOD FOR LUCK

No one knows for sure where the superstition of knocking on (or simply touching) wood for luck originated, but some believe the practice has ancient roots across several cultures. For example, some say it originated from the ancient pagan belief that spirits lived in trees and that knocking on wood could grant their protection; it was also considered a way to show gratitude for good fortune. In Christianity, this practice is linked to the cross upon which Jesus was crucified. Whatever its origins, knocking on wood has become a common gesture to ward off bad luck or ensure a positive outcome.

BREAKING A MIRROR BRINGS BAD LUCK

This superstition likely harkens back to ancient Rome, when it was believed that mirrors reflected a person's soul. Damaging a mirror would, therefore, harm that person's spiritual well-being. The seven-year duration also probably stems from the ancient Roman belief in cycles of renewal and rebirth. In the Middle Ages, mirrors were expensive and rare, so breaking one was viewed as a sign of impending misfortune or even death. This belief is perpetuated in many cultures today, as breaking a mirror is still considered one of the pinnacles of bad luck.

UNUSUAL SUPERSTITIONS

AVOID WALKING UNDER LADDERS

Walking under ladders has been associated with bad luck for centuries. In ancient Egypt, ladders were left in tombs to allow the spirits of the dead to ascend, and the triangle between the ladder, wall, and floor was thought to be filled with both good and evil spirits—who ought not to be disturbed. In medieval Europe, ladders leaned against the gallows, and walking under them became associated with tempting fate or even impending death. The Christian faith considers triangles as a symbol of the Holy Trinity (Father, Son, and Holy Spirit), so walking through the space under a ladder can be seen as a disruption of this sacred trio. Throughout the years, these beliefs merged, solidifying the taboo against walking under ladders, and the act is now synonymous with misfortune and bad luck.

A HORSESHOE FOR GOOD LUCK

As with many other superstitions, placing a horseshoe above a door for good luck can be traced back to ancient times and the belief that certain shapes held specific meanings. In this case, a horseshoe is shaped like a crescent moon, which was thought to ward off evil spirits. Iron has a long tradition as a protective metal, with the power to ward off evil spirits. While some considered it important to place the horseshoe with the ends pointing upward because it would catch and hold good fortune, others placed the open end down, allowing luck to pour over visitors to their homes.

THROWING SALT OVER THE LEFT SHOULDER

In ancient cultures, salt was a precious commodity believed to contain purifying qualities. When someone spilled salt, it was considered an unfortunate waste, potentially inviting evil spirits into that person's life. To keep that from happening, the person would toss some of the spilled salt over their left shoulder, where the devil was believed to lurk. The salt blinded the devil, negating any pending bad fortune. This superstition became common across numerous cultures, even after salt was no longer considered a luxury.

A FOUR-LEAF CLOVER FOR LUCK

The superstition of finding a four-leaf clover for luck has its roots in ancient Celtic lore and the belief that these rare clovers possess magical properties. Each leaf of a four-leaf clover symbolizes a desirable outcome: faith, hope, love, and luck. In Celtic culture, the number four was associated with protection and good fortune, which lent even more importance to finding a four-leaf clover amid the three-leaf variety. Those who found a four-leaf clover were considered blessed and protected from evil spirits, and some said that giving them away provided even more good fortune. Today, people still search for these elusive clovers, looking to bring luck and positivity into their lives.

CHAPTER TWELVE: POP CULTURE POTPOURRI

FUN FACTS ABOUT CELEBRITIES

TOM CRUISE'S REAL NAME

Tom Cruise was born Thomas Cruise Mapother IV on July 3, 1962. His surname, Mapother, comes from his father's side of the family, but Tom adopted "Cruise" as his stage name, dropping both Mapother and the IV suffix when he began his acting career. The Mapother surname originates in England, though Tom's family is Irish.

NICOLAS CAGE OWNED A PET OCTOPUS

While Nicolas Cage was filming the movie Ghost Rider in the early 2000s, he mentioned in several interviews that he'd owned a pet octopus in the mid-1980s—a reflection of his fascination with exotic animals, especially the octopus and its unusual high intelligence. Cage has long had a reputation for odd interests and behaviors, and his pet octopus just added to that perception. He named the octopus "Cool" and kept it in one of two aquariums in his Hollywood apartment.

STEVE BUSCEMI WAS A FIREFIGHTER

Prior to becoming an actor, Steve Buscemi served as a firefighter in New York City with Engine Company 55, serving for four years in the early 1980s. In the aftermath of the 9/11 terrorist attacks, Buscemi returned to his former firehouse to volunteer. Buscemi's experience as a firefighter continues to influence him today, as he has spoken at firefighter union rallies and hosted the HBO documentary *A Good Job: Stories of the FDNY*.

BETTY WHITE PREDATES SLICED BREAD

Betty White, an American Icon who passed away in 2021—just shy of 100 years old—was born on January 17, 1922, well before sliced bread was first sold to the public in 1928. In fact, at seven years old, White likely remembered the advent of sliced bread, as it marked the beginning of convenience foods. The phrase "the greatest thing since sliced bread" was popularized in the 1930s as the convenience of buying sliced bread instead of slicing it yourself was a monumental moment in culture.

ELVIS PRESLEY DYED HIS HAIR

Elvis Presley was known for his dark locks, but his hair was actually a sandy-blond color. While there have been rumors that he used black shoe polish to get his trademark jet-black hair, his hairdressers have said that he used regular commercial hair dye products to achieve his signature look. Whether polished or dyed, he began this practice early in his career to stand out on stage, believing the dark locks appealed more to his audiences.

STRANGE POP CULTURE PHENOMENA

EMBRACING ALL THINGS RETRO

Driven by nostalgia and the desire to reconnect with past eras, retro fashion returns in every generation as people seek to evoke a sense of familiarity and simplicity that retro fashion, music, design, and other objects represent. As the modern world grows increasingly fast-paced, retro trends offer a nostalgic escape that appeals to both older generations, as an opportunity to relive their youth, and younger generations, who enjoy discovering a different time. Retro aesthetics are celebrated for their timeless appeal and, frequently, their craftsmanship, often viewed as superior to modern materials and techniques.

INTERNET CHALLENGES

Internet challenges, such as the Ice Bucket Challenge of the mid-2010s—which raised millions of dollars for amyotrophic lateral sclerosis (ALS) research—combine simple and easily replicated tasks with social media's reach and a call to action for a cause. These tasks are generally simple, which makes them inclusive and accessible. Because content can spread quickly through shares, likes, and nominations, internet challenges have gained increasing popularity; being associated with a cause taps into the desire for altruism and doesn't require much effort, as just participating in the challenge brings awareness to causes that may not usually get much attention.

VIRAL TIKTOK DANCES

TikTok dances are easy to learn and replicate, making them accessible to people of all ages and skill levels. They're usually set to popular music across a wide range of audiences, so everyone can participate. Of course, in the digital age, TikTok's algorithm plays a major role in which dances go viral by promoting content that generates engagement. This algorithm amplifies each dance's reach, and the community aspect of TikTok encourages users to join in and create their own versions.

THE RISE OF ASMR

Autonomous sensory meridian response (ASMR) videos, named after the "tingling" sensation they evoke on the scalp that travels down the spine, have become immensely popular online. These clips feature various repetitive sounds and actions, such as tapping, whispering, or brushing, designed to gently evoke feelings of relaxation and euphoria. People seek out ASMR content to sleep better, reduce stress, or experience the frisson—also known as "aesthetic chills"—they inspire. YouTube creators have boosted the popularity of ASMR by creating customized experiences for diverse audiences and their preferences. The sensory experience provided the chance for millions of people to gain a heightened state of relaxation.

TRIVIA FROM MOVIES, TV, & BOOKS

THE OLDEST SURVIVING FILM

The "Roundhay Garden Scene," filmed by French inventor Louis Le Prince in 1888, is widely considered the first movie ever made. This short experimental film captured a few seconds of four people walking in a garden at Roundhay Park in Leeds, England. Despite its brevity, it's notable for its simplicity and historical significance, showcasing early motion picture technology using a single-lens camera.

THE LONGEST-RUNNING TV SHOW

Premiering in 1989, the animated sitcom The Simpsons stands as the longest-running TV series in history. Since the "actors" in the show never grow older, the show has a unique ability to evolve with societal changes while retaining its original humor and storytelling qualities. Writers cleverly parody contemporary issues in their storylines, making the show popular with all ages. With every new generation, The Simpsons adds to its fan base, ensuring its longevity and continued appeal.

TRANSLATED INTO OVER 80 LANGUAGES

J.K. Rowling's *Harry Potter* book series was translated into over 80 languages because of its universal themes of friendship and bravery, which resonate with readers worldwide. The added element of magic and the richly described wizarding world have captivated readers everywhere, and the characters and plotlines cross-cultural and language barriers, making the series accessible and beloved everywhere in the world. Harry Potter's cultural impact and subsequent film adaptations encouraged publishers to translate the books into as many languages as possible, ensuring that readers everywhere could experience the series' magic and adventure.

AN ORIGINAL NAME

F. Scott Fitzgerald's masterpiece *The Great Gatsby* was originally titled "Trimalchio in West Egg," a reference to a fictional Roman character known for his extravagant parties. Fitzgerald wanted to draw parallels between this pleasure-seeking character and the self-indulgent excesses of the 1920s Jazz Age. However, publishers believed the reference to Trimalchio too obscure for readers, so it was retitled *The Great Gatsby* to focus more on the central character of the book, Jay Gatsby. Ultimately, the marketing change made the book more appealing to general audiences, and eventually, the book became a staple of American literature.

RANDOM TIDBITS FROM THE WORLD OF ENTERTAINMENT

THE WILHELM SCREAM

Since the 1950s, the Wilhelm Scream has been used in hundreds of films. This stock sound effect of a man screaming was named after Private Wilhelm from the 1953 film *The Charge at Feather River* and gained cult popularity for its distinctive, comical quality, becoming something of an inside joke among filmmakers and audiences. Today, the Wilhelm Scream is more of an Easter egg, as directors like Steven Spielberg and George Lucas have incorporated the stock sound into films as a playful nod to cinema history and the shared experience of audiences across generations.

"JUMPING THE SHARK"

In 1977, Happy Day's character Fonzie literally jumped over a shark while on water skis, becoming the moment audiences pointed to as a sign the show had run its course. Since then, the phrase "jumping the shark" has been used to describe when a TV show or other creative work experiences a significant downturn in quality. Usually, the moment is characterized by a desperate or outlandish stunt designed to maintain viewership despite declining ratings. The phrase is now cultural shorthand for when something loses its authenticity or integrity, opting for gimmicks instead.

STAN LEE CAMEOS

Stan Lee, the co-creator of numerous Marvel characters, made cameo appearances in almost every Marvel movie, creating a game for audiences as they tried to spot him in the cast. For example, Lee played a security guard in *Captain America: The Winter Soldier*, a FedEx delivery man in *Avengers: Age of Ultron*, and a barber in *Thor: Ragnarok*. His last cameo in a Marvel movie, before he died in 2018, was in *Avengers: Endgame* as he drove a car past an army base, saying, "Hey, man. Make love, not war."

THE *FRIENDS* THEME SONG

The band R.E.M. wrote and recorded the song "Shiny Happy People" in September and October 1991. It was released as the second single from their seventh studio album, *Out of Time*. NBC approached the band to use this song as the theme to a new sitcom, *Friends*, but R.E.M. declined. Instead, the opportunity went to The Rembrandts, the only band that Warner Brothers had under contract at the time that was available to record a song. The Rembrandts wrote the 45-second "I'll Be There for You" strictly for the show's opener, but it became so popular that the band wrote two additional verses for the song, which eventually became a number one hit on Billboard's US Mainstream Top 40 list.

CHAPTER THIRTEEN: WEIRD SCIENCE

STRANGE PSYCHOLOGICAL EXPERIMENTS

THE MILGRAM EXPERIMENT

In the 1960s, psychologist Stanley Milgram conducted what would become known as the "Milgram Experiment," a controversial study of obedience to authority. Milgram instructed participants to administer an electric shock to a "learner" whenever they answered an incorrect question. The "learner" was actually an actor and the shocks fake, but participants believed they were real. The experiment found that people were willing to administer potentially harmful shocks when told to do so by an authority figure, highlighting the powerful influence of authority on human behavior, influencing ordinary people to commit acts they normally wouldn't.

THE STANFORD PRISON EXPERIMENT

In 1971, psychologist Philip Zimbardo led a study on the effects of perceived power in a simulated prison environment. The study, later called the "Stanford Prison Experiment," was scheduled to last two weeks, with Zimbardo assigning college students roles as either guards or prisoners in a mock prison. However, the study was terminated after just six days, as the "guards" began exhibiting abusive behavior toward the "prisoners." The experiment showed how significantly assigned roles and situational factors can influence human behavior. It also raised ethical questions about authority, conformity, and psychological research in general.

THE BOBO DOLL EXPERIMENT

In the early 1960s, psychologist Albert Bandura conducted a series of experiments to study the effects of observational learning on children's behavior. During the study, children watched an adult interact aggressively with a Bobo doll, a large inflatable toy. When allowed to play with the same doll later, the children who'd observed the abuse were more likely to imitate the behavior, displaying similar aggression. This experiment demonstrated that children learn and replicate behaviors just by watching others, highlighting the significant influence of role models and media on children's behavior.

THE MONSTER STUDY

In 1939, Wendell Johnson conducted the "Monster Study" at the University of Iowa to better understand the origins of stuttering. He divided 22 orphaned children into two groups; one group received praise for their speech, while the other was criticized for normal imperfections in their speech. The experiment found that negative therapy caused significant emotional harm and speech issues in children who previously had no problems at all. The study was condemned for its unethical methods and severe psychological impact, earning the experiment its monstrous name.

UNUSUAL SCIENTIFIC DISCOVERIES

PENICILLIN

In 1928, Scottish microbiologist Dr. Alexander Fleming accidentally discovered penicillin while working at St. Mary's Hospital in London. Fleming had noticed that a mold contaminated one of the petri dishes of Staphylococcus bacteria he'd been cultivating—but surprisingly the mold, which he identified as coming from the Penicillium family, killed the surrounding bacteria. When Fleming realized the mold produced a substance that could kill numerous types of bacteria, he conducted more studies to confirm his findings by growing more Penicillium. What he learned would revolutionize medicine, leading to the development of several antibiotics that have saved countless lives in the nearly 100 years since.

THE COSMIC MICROWAVE

Arno Penzias and Robert Wilson, two radio astronomers at Bell Labs, discovered the cosmic microwave background (CMB) radiation in 1964. Penzias and Wilson were testing a sensitive antenna when they encountered a persistent noise they could not eliminate. They ruled out all possible sources of interference before realizing they had discovered something completely new and extraordinary. The radiation, which was uniform in all directions, was determined to be the afterglow of the Big Bang, providing strong evidence for this theory of the universe's creation. Penzias and Wilson earned the 1978 Nobel Prize in Physics for their accidental discovery.

THE HIGGS BOSON PARTICLE

Often referred to as the "God Particle," the Higgs boson particle was discovered by physicists at CERN's Large Hadron Collider (LHC) in Switzerland on July 4, 2012. Although physicists had theorized the existence of the Higgs boson particle for years, they were never able to observe it until the LHC, the world's most powerful particle accelerator, caused protons to collide at high speeds, giving the scientists a glimpse of the elusive Higgs boson. This discovery confirmed the theory that particles gain mass through interactions with the Higgs field, a theory that Peter Higgs and other scientists proposed as early as the 1960s. The discovery earned a Nobel Prize in Physics in 2013.

THE FIRST EXOPLANET

Astronomers Aleksander Wolszczan and Dale Frail discovered the first exoplanet—or planet outside the solar system—in 1992. Named PSR B1257+12, the exoplanet orbits a pulsar, a type of neutron star, in the constellation Virgo. This significant discovery proved that planets could exist around stars completely different from the Sun. It also challenged existing theories about planet formation, opening up the possibility of finding habitable worlds beyond our solar system.

DYNAMITE

In 1847, Ascanio Sobrero, an Italian chemist, invented nitroglycerin. He later discovered that combining glycerol with nitric and sulfuric acids produced an explosive compound far more powerful than gunpowder. It was also much more volatile. Sobrero did not want his invention to get out because he feared its use. However, his lab mate, Alfred Nobel, saw the potential in the explosive compound for creating profitable weapons and other explosives. Twenty years after the invention of nitroglycerin, Nobel invented dynamite, blowing up two of his factories in the process.

WARFARIN

The benefits of many drugs have been accidentally discovered while being tested for other uses, but warfarin, a popular blood thinner, was not discovered in a lab but in a livestock field. In the 1920s, cattle and sheep began dying from internal bleeding after grazing on moldy hay. Some animals also began bleeding to death after routine veterinary procedures. Canadian veterinarian Frank Schofield found that the mold on the hay contained an anticoagulant that prevented the livestock's blood from clotting. In 1940, biochemist Karl Link and his team at the University of Wisconsin isolated the anticoagulant compound and created warfarin, named after the Wisconsin Alumni Research Foundation (WARF), which funded the drug's development.

QUIRKY SCIENTIFIC THEORIES

THE MULTIVERSE THEORY

This theory proposes that the universe is just one of many infinite possible universes that exist simultaneously. These parallel universes could have different physical laws, constants, and even entirely different realities. The multiverse theory results from several scientific theories, such as quantum mechanics, cosmic inflation, and string theory. Essentially, the theory states that every decision a person makes creates a new universe, where each possible outcome of that decision occurs. The theory, while intriguing, isn't based on any direct evidence, but it has sparked debates about alternate realities among scientists and fans of science fiction.

THE SIMULATION HYPOTHESIS

This theory proposes that reality as we perceive it might actually be a computer simulation—basically, that we are characters in a highly-advanced virtual reality created by an equally-advanced civilization. The hypothesis raises philosophical questions about the nature of existence and consciousness, suggesting that our entire universe could be an intricate simulation. Believers in this theory argue that technological advancements may one day allow us to create such advanced simulations ourselves, blurring the lines between what is real and what is simulated.

THE PARALLEL UNIVERSE THEORY

Similar to the multiverse theory, this quirky theory suggests that our universe may be just one of numerous universes existing at the same time. These universes may vary in physical constants, laws of nature, or even the fundamental forces governing them. This theory is popular among science fiction writers and fans, where alternate realities exist with different versions of ourselves, and our lives based on alternative choices.

THE PANSPERMIA THEORY

The panspermia theory suggests that life exists throughout the universe, distributed between planets, moons, and solar systems through comets, asteroids, or other celestial bodies. The theory proposes that life's building blocks, such as amino acids and microorganisms, can travel through space and create life on other celestial bodies. It's considered more of a spiritual theory, challenging the idea that life only originates from within a planet or moon and suggesting a cosmic interconnectedness. As with the other theories presented here, the panspermia theory remains speculative, but ongoing research continues to explore the idea that life could survive the harsh environment of space travel.

FUN SCIENCE EXPERIMENTS

BAKING SODA & VINEGAR VOLCANO

To create this classic science experiment, first build a volcano shape using a base like clay or a plastic bottle. Mix baking soda with a few drops of dish soap inside the base, then pour vinegar into the "volcano's" crater. Acid in the vinegar will react with the base in baking soda to produce carbon dioxide, resulting in a foamy eruption that resembles lava—especially if you add a few drops of red food coloring! Keep experimenting with different quantities of baking soda and vinegar to observe various eruption effects. This simple experiment demonstrates one of the most basic chemical reactions in a safe and controlled environment.

SLIME

A few years ago, making slime was all the rage among elementary and middle school children, but this fun activity is a wonderful science experiment resulting in a tactile and sensory experience. Start by mixing equal parts of white school glue and water in a bowl. In a separate bowl, dissolve a teaspoon of borax powder in a cup of warm water. Slowly pour the borax solution into the glue mixture while stirring continuously. As you mix the concoction, the slime will begin to form. Once you can pick it up without it dripping all over the place, knead and stretch the slime with your hands until it reaches the desired consistency.

HOMEMADE ELECTROMAGNETS

To build a homemade electromagnet, you'll need insulated copper wire, an iron nail, and a battery. Wrap the insulated copper wire tightly around the nail, leaving the two ends of the wire free.

Connect the ends of the wire to the battery. When the electrical current flows through the wire, it will generate a magnetic field around the nail, transforming it into an electromagnet. You can use the electromagnet to pick up small metal objects like paper clips and pushpins. Experiment with the number of wire coils around the nail and different battery strengths to increase the magnetic force.

GROWING CRYSTALS

Choose a crystal-forming substance, such as salt or sugar. Prepare a supersaturated solution of your chosen crystal-forming substance by dissolving it in hot water. Pour this solution into a clean glass or clear jar and suspend a seed crystal from a string or fishing line into the solution. The seed crystal should be a small crystal of either salt or sugar, whichever you use in the solution. Place the container in a cool, undisturbed location and watch as crystals slowly form over the next several days and weeks.

CHAPTER FOURTEEN: LITERATURE LOO BREAK

FUN FACTS ABOUT FAMOUS AUTHORS

MARK TWAIN'S REAL NAME

Mark Twain, one of America's most beloved authors, wrote under a pen name. His real name was Samuel Langhorne Clements, but he chose to use the pen name to separate his literary pursuits from his earlier, less successful ventures. He originally wrote under his birth name, but struggled, suffering significant financial setbacks. The pseudonym was inspired by his riverboat days on the Mississippi River, where the phrase "mark twain" indicated safe waters. The pen name allowed Twain to start fresh and distance himself from his past failures, and eventually, the name became synonymous with wit, humor, and insightful storytelling.

AGATHA CHRISTIE'S FIRST JOB

In 1915, detective novelist Agatha Christie worked as an apothecary's assistant in Torquay's Red Cross Hospital pharmacy. There, Christie learned both the theoretical and practical aspects of chemistry and became well-informed about various poisons, which would later become central to her crime and mystery novels. She used her knowledge of medicines and poisons to lay the groundwork for her meticulous attention to detail in her plots. Her exposure to various pharmaceuticals fueled Christie's fascination with crime and detection, leading her to pursue her true calling as a novelist.

HARRY POTTER STARTED ON NAPKINS

Despite internet rumors that J.K. Rowling was so poor when she was writing the first Harry Potter book that she had to write it on napkins, she later said in an interview, "No, I did not write on napkins. I could afford pens and paper." However, Rowling did jot down ideas on scraps of paper, including napkins—and even airplane "barf bag"—as she went through the writing process. Rowling has said that the initial spark for the *Harry Potter* stories came during a delayed train journey, where she imagined a young wizard traveling on a train to attend a school of magic.

ERNEST HEMINGWAY SURVIVED

The myth that Ernest Hemingway survived multiple plane crashes during his life is true, but only just; he was only involved in two plane crashes. In 1954, while on a sightseeing expedition in Africa, the small plane Hemingway and his wife were in crashed in the Belgian Congo. The very next day, after spending a night in the jungle, Hemingway's plane crashed just after takeoff. Hemingway suffered injuries in both crashes, despite headlines reporting his death. Unfortunately, the injuries negatively affected his health, contributing to numerous ongoing physical ailments and alcoholism, both of which plagued him the rest of his life.

STRANGE LITERARY TRIVIA

THE WORD "SERENDIPITY"

English writer and fourth Earl of Orford Horace Walpole coined the word "serendipity" in a letter to a friend in 1754. The word was inspired by a "silly fairy tale," The Three Princes of Serendip, in which characters made discoveries by accident. Walpole was fascinated by the princes' tendency to find things they weren't seeking, and "serendipity" came to mean a fortunate discovery stumbled upon by chance. While its original meaning has been considered rather mundane by some, the word eventually became synonymous with unexpected discoveries or fortunate accidents and has since gained an almost mystical quality.

SHAKESPEARE INVENTED OVER 1,700 WORDS

Though scholars don't know the exact number of unique words Shakespeare coined, he's credited with the creation of over 1,700 words still in common use today. Shakespeare's innovative use of language included inventing new words, adapting existing words, and creatively combining roots and prefixes to create new meanings. Examples of words attributed to Shakespeare include "bedazzled," "swagger," "dwindle," "gloomy," and "lonely." These additions expanded the English vocabulary and demonstrated Shakespeare's incredible influence on the evolution of language.

A COMMERCIAL FAILURE

When F. Scott Fitzgerald's masterpiece, *The Great Gatsby*, was first released in 1925, it was a major commercial disappointment. However, in the 1940s, World War II brought about a renewed interest in American literature, and critics revived the novel, bringing attention to the evergreen themes of wealth, ambition, and the American Dream. The novel's critique of societal values and the excesses of the Jazz Age resonated with readers and solidified it as an American classic. Today, the book is celebrated for its symbolism and portrayal of America in the "Roaring Twenties."

WRITTEN ON A BET

The rumor that Dr. Seuss wrote *Green Eggs and Ham* on a bet is partially true. As the story goes, Dr. Seuss's editor, Bennett Cerf, challenged the writer to write a book using only fifty different words. As such, the book was the result of more of a personal challenge than an actual wager. However, Cerf's motivation was to create a marketable book that would encourage children to read, and Seuss met the challenge, writing what would become a beloved children's classic, demonstrating his ability to craft an engaging and fun story with a limited vocabulary. Green Eggs and Ham went on to become one of the best-selling English-language children's books in history.

OBSCURE BOOK RECOMMENDATIONS

HOUSE OF LEAVES

Mark Z. Danielewski's debut book, *House of Leaves*, is a complex novel written in an unconventional style. It explores a house defying spatial logic and uses footnotes, different typographies, and narrative styles. Readers who enjoy psychological thrillers, puzzles, and experimental literature are bound to enjoy this book, which challenges the perception of reality and ideas of fear, obsession, and the supernatural. Its innovative structure appeals to readers with a thought-provoking and immersive reading experience that blurs the lines between reality and fiction.

THE MASTER AND MARGARITA

The Russian novel *The Master and Margarita* by Mikhail Bulgakov is set in Soviet Moscow and tells the story of Satan visiting the city while interweaving a retelling of the story of Jesus and Pontius Pilate. Bulgakov's writing blends political satire, fantasy, and philosophical exploration to create a novel rich with dark humor, intricate plots, and religious allegories. The themes of love, redemption, and the nature of good and evil are present throughout the story, even as Bulgakov focuses on critiquing totalitarianism. Readers who enjoy thought-provoking novels will enjoy this work of Russian literature.

THE NIGHT CIRCUS

Erin Morgenstern's novel *The Night Circus* tells the tale of a magical competition between two young illusionists bound by fate and love. It's set in a mystical, black-and-white circus that appears without warning, weaving together elements of romance, intrigue, and fantasy. Readers who enjoy enchanting prose, intricate storytelling, and vivid imagery will be captivated by this blend of romance and mystery set in a whimsical and magical world.

THE LIBRARY AT MOUNT CHAR

The difficult-to-categorize novel *The Library at Mount Char* by Scott Hawkins is a dark and inventive fantasy that tells the story of Carolyn, one of twelve orphaned children raised by a mysterious figure known as "Father." Each child must master a different catalog of knowledge in a massive, otherworldly library. Carolyn begins to unravel the secrets of the library and recognize her own powers as the story explores the themes of family, power, and the nature of knowledge. Readers who enjoy genre-bending novels, complex characters, and twisted plots will find this book thoroughly thrilling and thought-provoking.

LITERARY QUOTES & THEIR ORIGINS

SHAKESPEARE

The quote "To be, or not to be, that is the question" is found in Act 3, Scene 1 of William Shakespeare's play *Hamlet*. In this scene, Prince Hamlet delivers a soliloquy in which he contemplates the nature of existence and the struggles of life, debating whether it's better to endure the hardships of life or end them all through death. The speech explores mortality, existentialism, and the complexities of human emotion. As such, it's one of the most famous and enduring passages in English literature, and the quote itself has become synonymous with internal human conflict and philosophical musings.

JANE AUSTEN

Jane Austen's classic novel *Pride and Prejudice* opens with the line "It is a truth universally acknowledged, that a single man in possession of a good fortune, must be in want of a wife." Published in 1813, the story examines the themes of love, marriage, and social status in 19th-century England. This quote humorously sets the tone for the book's exploration of societal expectations, including the pursuit of marriage among the British social class of landowners called the "landed gentry." It's one of the most famous opening lines in English literature.

GEORGE ORWELL

In George Orwell's allegorical novel *Animal Farm,* published in 1945, a pig (the story's ruling class) proclaims, "All animals are equal, but some animals are more equal than others." In the story, a group of farm animals overthrow their human farmer to pursue equality and self-governance. Over time, the pigs manipulate the original "commandments" of equality to justify their own privileges and power. In essence, they speak about equality among everyone else but treat themselves as "more equal" and thereby deserving of more privileges. The quote is a satirical commentary on the hypocrisy of totalitarian regimes and the tendency to betray revolutionary ideals such as equality.

CHARLES DICKENS

The English classic *A Tale of Two Cities* by Charles Dickens opens with the quote, "It was the best of times, it was the worst of times." Published in 1859, the novel is set during the French Revolution, a time of turbulence and uncertainty. The book contrasts the realities of life in London and Paris, using the quote to illustrate the dualities and contradictions of human existence. In every situation, there is hope and despair, joy and sorrow—two very different sides of the same coin. The novel explores these dichotomies and how they reflect the complexities of society and the human condition.

CHAPTER FIFTEEN: HEALTH & WELLNESS WONDERS

UNUSUAL HEALTH TIPS & TRICKS

OIL PULLING FOR DENTAL HEALTH

The practice of oil pulling stems from the ancient Ayurvedic tradition of swishing a tablespoon of coconut, sesame, or sunflower oil in your mouth for about fifteen minutes before spitting it out. It's believed that this practice removes toxins from the mouth, improves oral hygiene, and whitens teeth. Essentially, the theory is that the oil "pulls" bacteria and plaque from the teeth and gums, removing these harmful elements from the body. While its benefits are not scientifically proven, it could reduce the number of harmful bacteria in your mouth.

COLD WATER THERAPY

Exposing the body to cold water is believed to improve circulation, causing blood vessels to constrict, then dilate, which then produces better blood flow. Cold water therapy is also said to reduce inflammation, boost the immune system, and release endorphins, resulting in an improved mood. Athletes, in particular, often use cold water therapy to reduce discomfort and muscle soreness, especially after intense competitions and workouts. The initial shock of an ice bath can be uncomfortable, but some insist that regular exposure to cold water can lead to improved circulation, among other health benefits, though there is no scientific evidence to support this.

EARTHING

Also known as "grounding," earthing involves making direct physical contact with the Earth's surface, usually by walking barefoot on grass, sand, or dirt. The idea is that the Earth's electrons interact with your skin to reduce inflammation, improve sleep, and boost your overall well-being. Advocates of earthing believe that people who always walk in shoes are insulated from the natural connection with the Earth, which may lead to sickness and a general sense of malaise. Currently, there is limited scientific evidence to support this theory, but the skin-to-earth connection does seem to provide some relief from stress.

BREATHING EXERCISES

You've probably been told to practice breathing exercises to help you relax, but do you know why that is? These exercises activate the parasympathetic nervous system, which counters the stress response in your body. Taking deep, slow breaths tells your brain it's time to calm down, reducing the production of stress hormones like cortisol. Deep breathing techniques bring more oxygen into your bloodstream, lowering your heart rate and blood pressure. Additionally, when you're focusing on your breathing, you aren't focusing on the stressors in your life, which can promote a sense of mindfulness and relaxation.

WEIRD MEDICAL CONDITIONS

ALIEN HAND SYNDROME

Alien hand syndrome is a rare neurological disorder that causes a person's hand to move and act on its own. The movements are out of the person's control and are often purposeful movements, such as buttoning a shirt or picking up items without the person wanting to. The condition typically appears after brain surgery, strokes, or neurodegenerative diseases that affect the brain's hemispheres. People who suffer from alien hand syndrome often describe their hand as "possessed" or alien to them, which is how it got its name. The condition can be distressing but usually improves through therapy and rehabilitation.

EXPLODING HEAD SYNDROME

Exploding head syndrome is a sleep disorder that results in a person hearing a loud, sudden noise just as they're falling asleep or waking up. The condition itself isn't dangerous and won't cause any physical harm to the sufferer, but it can be distressing and make it harder for the person to fall asleep, fearing they'll hear the noises again. Sometimes, the noises are accompanied by flashes of light, which are also entirely imagined. The sounds and lights are thought to be caused by sudden shifts in the brain's activity during the transition between wakefulness and sleep.

CAPGRAS DELUSION

Named after the French psychiatrist Joseph Capgras, the rare psychiatric disorder Capgras delusion is when a person believes that someone close to them, usually a family member or friend, has been replaced by an identical impostor. Capgras first described the disorder in 1923 as a delusion often associated with schizophrenia, dementia, or brain injury. Although the exact cause is unknown, today, it's thought to involve a disconnect between the brain's facial recognition processes and the emotional response that familiar faces normally trigger. The symptoms of Capgras delusion can be improved through antipsychotic medications and therapy.

FOREIGN ACCENT SYNDROME

The rare, strange medical condition called foreign accent syndrome causes a person to suddenly begin speaking with a different accent, usually described as "foreign," without having been influenced by actually visiting the apparent place of its origin. FAS typically occurs after a brain injury or stroke that has damaged the brain's speech center. The sufferer doesn't intend to change their accent, which makes it extremely distressing for them. They not only don't understand why they're doing it, but it can also lead to other psychological and social challenges. Promising treatments usually focus on speech or music therapy, though the rarity of the disorder has made it difficult to study.

STRANGE WELLNESS PRACTICES

FOREST BATHING

Shinrin-yoku, or forest bathing, is a Japanese ritual of immersing oneself in nature to improve health and mental well-being. The practice involves walking mindfully and slowly through a forest, engaging all the senses to connect with the natural environment. Forest bathing began in the 1980s to counteract the stress that came with Japan's urbanization. Research suggests that forest bathing lowers blood pressure, reduces the production of stress hormones, boosts immunity, and improves mood. This popular wellness activity has helped people feel more relaxed and rejuvenated for decades in Japan, and people in other countries are beginning to adopt it.

LAUGHTER YOGA

Dr. Madan Kataria introduced the practice of laughter yoga in India in 1995, believing that, because the body can't differentiate between fake and real laughter, forced laughter provides the same wellness benefits as real laughter. The practice involves group yoga sessions that include laughing for no reason, which soon becomes genuine and contagious. Eventually, everyone in the group is laughing genuinely, gaining the physiological and psychological benefits laughter provides. The goals of laughter yoga include reducing stress, improving mood, and boosting immunity, but it also focuses on strengthening social connections through shared laughter.

FIRE CUPPING THERAPY

Fire cupping therapy is a traditional Asian practice that involves placing heated bamboo or glass cups upside-down onto a person's skin to create a suction effect as the cup cools. Cupping is believed to stimulate blood flow, relieve muscle tension, and promote accelerated healing by drawing toxins out of the body. Practitioners use fire to heat the cups, then place them on specific acupuncture points on the body. As the cups cool down, they create a vacuum that pulls the skin into the cup, supposedly removing toxins or "stagnant blood." Cupping is often used to treat pain, inflammation, and respiratory issues.

WATSU

Watsu, a therapeutic practice conducted in warm water pools, combines the elements of shiatsu massage and stretching. Participants gently stretch their bodies while floating in warm water. The buoyancy of the water reduces joint strain, which allows for deeper relaxation and increased flexibility. The goals of Watsu (also known as "water shiatsu") are to release tension, improve circulation, and promote a deep sense of relaxation and well-being. Watsu was originally developed by Harold Dull, an American aquatic bodywork therapist, in the 1980s, to take advantage of the relaxing and healing benefits of warm water environments.

FUN FACTS ABOUT THE HUMAN BODY

- Your stomach lining replaces itself every few days
- Humans shed about 600,000 particles of skin every hour
- The strongest muscle, based on weight, in the human body, is the masseter (jaw muscle)
- Your nose can remember 50,000 different scents
- Beards grow faster than any other hair on the human body
- Everyone has a unique tongue print, which can be used to identify them
- The nail on the middle finger of each hand grows faster than any other nail
- Sneezes can reach speeds of over 100 miles per hour, while coughs can reach speeds of about sixty miles per hour

- Humans spend about 3 to 8 percent of their waking hours with their eyes closed because they're blinking
- Each human produces enough saliva to fill about five hundred bathtubs in a lifetime
- The small intestine can grow up to 23 feet long, about three times longer than a person's average height
- Stomach acid is so strong that it can cause metal to rust
- The sciatic nerve, which runs from the spinal cord to the toes, is the longest nerve in the body
- The human brain is made of 60 percent fat
- The average human has 67 different bacteria species in their belly button
- Human teeth are as strong as shark teeth
- Blood makes up 8 percent of a human's body weight, and skin makes up 15 percent of a human's body weight

CHAPTER SIXTEEN: MYTHBUSTING MOMENTS

DEBUNKING COMMON MYTHS

HUMANS ONLY USE 10% OF THEIR BRAINS

It's often said that humans only use 10 percent of their brains, but this is a myth. It probably came from early misinterpretations of neuroscience and brain imaging. More recent studies show that most parts of the brain are active at different times, even during routine activities. It's true that some of our brain's potential might remain untapped, but it's far from 90 percent, and it might be as little as less than 1 percent. Neuroscience indicates that the human brain is highly active and efficient in managing cognitive functions.

CHEWING GUM SURVIVES SEVEN YEARS

The human digestive system is designed to process and eliminate even the most indigestible of substances, including gum, so the claim that if you swallow chewing gum, it will stay in your stomach for seven years is false. It probably originated from parents who didn't want their children to swallow their gum. It's true that gum base is resistant to digestive enzymes, but it's expelled from the body—and into the toilet!—within a few days, not years. As long as you don't do it on a regular basis, swallowing chewing gum doesn't pose any health risks.

CRACKING KNUCKLES CAUSES ARTHRITIS

Although cracking your knuckles might be annoying to some, it doesn't increase your risk of developing arthritis. Research has proven that habitual knuckle cracking doesn't cause any joint damage, either—the sound you hear when you crack your knuckles is just the bursting of gas bubbles that build up in your joints' synovial fluid, a substance that lubricates the joints. The myth persists because the cracking noise doesn't sound healthy, but in truth, it's completely harmless.

GOLDFISH HAVE A 3-SECOND MEMORY

Even though goldfish don't have the best memory, it lasts longer than three seconds. Research has shown that goldfish can remember things for weeks, months, or even years, and can be trained to respond to light cues for food. Of course, memory span varies from fish to fish—just as it does from human to human. Some goldfish have learned to navigate mazes, recognize different people, and remember feeding schedules. The myth probably came about because goldfish display repetitive behaviors that may appear to lack memory but have no connection to their cognitive abilities.

URBAN LEGENDS EXPLAINED

THE HOOKMAN

There are several variations of the Hookman urban legend, but most tales tell of a couple parked in a remote area that hears a news report about an escaped criminal with a hook for a hand that may be in the vicinity. Fearful, the couple leaves quickly, but when they get home, they find a bloody hook hanging from their car door handle. The story isn't true, but it does tap into fears of isolated places, unknown dangers, and the vulnerability of young people in remote places. The legend is probably a cautionary tale to discourage teenagers from engaging in risky behavior.

THE VANISHING HITCHHIKER

As with the Hookman legend, the vanishing hitchhiker legend has numerous variations. Generally, it involves a driver picking up a hitchhiker who mysteriously disappears from the car during the drive. The driver later learns that the hitchhiker was the ghost of someone who died in a car accident near where they were picked up. The serves as a warning about picking up strangers, and details change based on local fears about travel, the unknown, and the supernatural.

THE KILLER IN THE BACKSEAT

Also known as "High Beams," this legend involves a driver who becomes aware of a dangerous—often murderous—presence in their car, usually after receiving a warning at a gas station or another car following them and flashing their headlights. The driver turns to find someone in the backseat. This person then kills the driver, giving rise to the name of the legend. There are many variations of the story, but it reminds drivers to stay aware of their surroundings, especially when alone or traveling at night.

THE BLOODY MARY LEGEND

The Bloody Mary legend revolves around a ritual in which participants repeatedly chant "Bloody Mary" in front of a mirror in an attempt to summon a ghostly apparition of a woman named Mary, who is said to have either died violently or had others killed. The ritual is a popular game at sleepovers and other gatherings of youths to test their bravery and that of their friends. In some versions of the story, Bloody Mary appears to those who call her name, often with horrifying consequences. The spooky story plays on fears of the unknown and supernatural.

FUN FACTS THAT CHALLENGE COMMON BELIEFS

THE GREAT WALL OF CHINA

The Great Wall of China is huge, stretching over 13,000 miles from Mount Hu near Dandong to the Jiayu Pass in the Gansu Province, but it's relatively narrow and made of materials that cause it to blend into its surroundings. As such, it is a myth that it's visible from space to the naked eye. In fact, astronauts have reported that the wall isn't visible without magnification, even from low orbit. Pictures of the Great Wall have been taken from satellites and specialized cameras from space, but these devices magnify the area to display structures that can't be seen by the naked eye alone.

LIGHTNING NEVER STRIKES THE SAME PLACE

Lightning can and does strike in the same location more than once, often repeatedly, especially tall structures or prominent natural features. Lighting takes the path of least resistance when it travels between the sky and Earth's surface, which means that certain structures and objects are more prone to attract lightning than others. Additionally, lightning rods and other conductive objects are actually designed to attract lighting strikes to protect people and buildings, absorbing multiple strikes over time. Even people can be struck by lightning more than once, thoroughly debunking this myth.

CHAMELEONS MEAN TO BLEND

While chameleons change color, it usually isn't for camouflage; instead, their skin changes color in response to various environmental factors, such as temperature and light. There's also evidence that they change their color based on their mood and to communicate with other chameleons, using their color-changing abilities to express emotions like stress or aggression or to warn other chameleons to stay away. While they do change color to blend into their surroundings occasionally, but it's not the primary purpose of this unique ability.

BATS ARE BLIND

Despite the popularity of the phrase "blind as a bat," bats aren't blind and have relatively good eyesight. Vision sensitivity varies among the different bat species, but most can see pretty well, though they rely more on their auditory senses. The idea that bats are blind rose from their use of echolocation, a unique ability that uses sound to navigate in complete darkness. This sophisticated sonar system allows them to perceive their surroundings with great accuracy, but it complements their eyesight rather than replaces it.

SCIENTIFIC EXPLANATIONS FOR PHENOMENA

BALL LIGHTNING

Numerous people have reported seeing balls of lightning during thunderstorms, but because ball lightning is rare and unpredictable, scientists have been unable to determine exactly what causes it and why it appears when it does. However, hypotheses suggest ball lightning forms when lighting strikes and vaporizes materials like silicon in the ground. The vapor then condenses into a floating plasma ball that can last from a few seconds to a few minutes, sustained by electromagnetic fields. In the absence of a scientific explanation for this phenomenon, some have suggested alien or supernatural involvement, especially since these balls are sometimes reported to pass through solid objects before disappearing.

SPONTANEOUS HUMAN COMBUSTION

Spontaneous human combustion (SHC) is a rare phenomenon where a human body supposedly catches fire without being exposed to an external ignition source. It's controversial and poorly understood, even by the scientific community. While most scientists are skeptical that SHC actually occurs and believe there are nearby external heat sources to explain the fire, some experts propose that SHC occurs due to an internal buildup of flammable gasses in the intestines. They suspect that clothing acts as a wick and static electricity acts as the source of ignition. With no controlled experiments, though, the actual cause remains a mystery.

CROP CIRCLES

Despite claims of supernatural or alien origins, most crop circles are human-made. They're usually created by artists or pranksters using simple tools like ropes and planks to flatten crops in geometric patterns. Crop circles almost always appear in areas accessible to the public and are more common during the summer months, when crops are tall. No credible evidence exists to support the fringe theories that aliens make crop circles. Time-lapse videos are available online, showing how people create these geometric patterns.

THE BERMUDA TRIANGLE

Located in the western part of the North Atlantic Ocean, the Bermuda Triangle has gained notoriety for being the location of several mysterious disappearances of ships and aircraft. However, most scientists believe that a combination of natural factors is responsible for the disappearances that happen to coincide frequently in this area. For example, unpredictable weather patterns, such as sudden storms and massive rogue waves, are common here, as are magnetic anomalies that confuse navigational instruments and can result in crashes. Methane gas eruptions from this part of the ocean floor may also disrupt buoyancy and propulsion systems. However, statistical analysis shows the rate of disappearances in the Bermuda Triangle is no higher than any other highly traveled ocean area in other parts of the world.

CHAPTER SEVENTEEN: THE GREAT OUTDOORS

CAMPING & SURVIVAL TIPS

CHOOSING THE RIGHT CAMPING GEAR

While choosing the right camping gear depends on your camping environment, some guidelines can help you shop for appropriate equipment. The tent you select needs to be suitable for the area's weather and climate, as should your sleeping bag. Be sure to bring a reliable camping stove, cookware, and multiple clothing layers to account for temperature changes. Pack a headlamp, flashlight, matches and/or other fire source, first aid kit, maps, compass, and multitool. Remember that quality gear is the key to survival, so plan to invest a significant amount of money in your equipment to make sure it suits your camping style and location.

BUILDING A FIRE SAFELY

To safely build a campfire, choose a clear, open spot away from overhanging branches, dry grass, or any of your camping gear. Clear a circle of ground and surround it with rocks. Gather tinder (dry grass, bark, etc.), kindling (small, dry branches, dead leaves, pine needles, etc.), and larger logs in separate piles. Place a small amount of tinder in the center of the circle and light it. Add more tinder gradually until flames are established. Then, add kindling, allowing the flames to grow. Finally, larger logs should be added to keep the fire burning. Never leave your fire unattended, and ensure it's fully extinguished with water and dirt before leaving your campsite.

FINDING & PURIFYING WATER

To find water when camping or in a survival situation, look for natural sources like streams, rivers, or lakes. If you don't have GPS or a map, look for clusters of trees or animal tracks to follow to a body of water. Always boil water over a fire or stove to kill bacteria and parasites before using it to cook or drink. It's also advisable to carry water purification tablets or a portable filter system to remove contaminants if you can't build a fire. Use these items according to the instructions before drinking the water to ensure the chemicals or filters have time to work.

NAVIGATING WITH A MAP & COMPASS

To navigate through an unfamiliar place, lay your map flat and align it with the surrounding terrain using landmarks. Use your compass to determine the direction or bearing to your destination or a landmark. Hold the compass steady and walk in the direction of the bearing. Check your compass periodically to make sure you're staying on track. Continuously adjust your course based on the terrain and landmarks and take time to periodically reorient the map to make sure your navigation is accurate. Practice navigating with a compass and map before using it in real-life situations.

WILD OUTDOOR ADVENTURES

SANDBOARDING ON DESERT DUNES

Sandboarding is similar to snowboarding, making the popular winter sport accessible throughout the year. Desert dunes create a dynamic landscape for thrill seekers, offering riders different slopes and unlimited challenges. People who don't live in areas where snowboarding is available can enjoy this sport by transferring it to the sand, and people who miss snowboarding in the summer can take their skills to a new level by testing their abilities in the desert. Sandboarding is popular in places like the Great Sand Dunes National Park in Colorado, the Oregon Dunes National Recreation Area, and the White Sands National Monument in New Mexico.

ICE CLIMBING ON GLACIERS

Mountain climbers who want to take their sport to a new level may want to consider ice climbing on glaciers. This activity is physically and mentally demanding as climbers scale frozen cascades and ice formations. The sport not only requires skill, strength, and strategic planning but also demands mental fortitude and the ability to adapt to changing circumstances as the ice melts or breaks off. Most ice climbing occurs in cold-weather regions like the Alps, Andes, and the Arctic, where the formations are more stable, creating a safer climbing adventure.

TREE CANOPY TOURS

Ziplining through forests has become an extremely popular activity for people traveling through places like Costa Rica, the Amazon, and other tropical rainforests throughout the world. However, it's also popular in other mountainous regions and forested areas. It offers a unique perspective of the forests, allowing participants to experience nature from a bird's-eye view as they soar above the canopy. The combination of exhilaration and connecting with nature make ziplining and canopy tours a favorite activity for anyone who seeks a fun and unique experience.

PARAGLIDING OFF MOUNTAIN PEAKS

Paragliding is a popular activity in mountainous regions where people can jump from high points. The Swiss Alps, Himalayas, and the Andes are prime locations for paragliders who want to launch themselves off a high-altitude cliff and glide through the air using a lightweight, free-flying canopy. Soaring like a bird while taking in stunning aerial views gives them a sense of freedom they can't get anywhere else. While major destinations such as those mentioned above are excellent places to paraglide, you can participate in this activity wherever there is an elevated area to safely jump from, as long as you abide by the area's regulations.

FUN FACTS ABOUT THE WILDERNESS

- Electric eels can produce an electric shock of up to 600 volts

- Bananas are berries, but strawberries are not
- A group of flamingos is called a flamboyance
- Giraffe tongues can be up to twenty inches long
- The blue whale has a heart the size of a small car
- Honeybees communicate with each other through a series of dance moves, one of which is called the "waggle dance," which conveys information about the location of food
- Axolotls can regenerate entire limbs, spinal cords, hearts, and other organs
- Redwood trees can reach heights of up to 350 feet
- A single bolt of lightning can reach temperatures as high as 30,000 Kelvin or 53,540 degrees Fahrenheit—hotter than the surface of the sun
- Volcanic lightning occurs when volcanic eruptions produce ash clouds, generating lightning strikes

OUTDOOR SKILLS & ACTIVITIES

WILDERNESS SURVIVAL TRAINING

Learning to survive in the wilderness is a skill that may seem irrelevant if you never go camping or hiking. However, it's an essential skill that can come in handy in numerous situations, not just camping and hiking. Knowing how to build shelters, find and purify water, start fires, and navigate unfamiliar terrain can save your life in emergencies. For example, if your vehicle runs out of gas or has a mechanical issue in the middle of nowhere, you might have to survive a few days before being rescued. Additionally, wilderness survival training boosts confidence, problem-solving abilities, and resilience, which are critical in times of chaos.

BUSHCRAFT & PRIMITIVE SKILLS

Bushcraft and primitive skills take your wilderness survival training to the next level as you learn to use natural resources for shelter, fire, and food. Not only do these skills ensure your survival in isolated areas, but they also allow you to connect with nature on a deep level. You'll also feel a strong sense of accomplishment when you learn to thrive in nature with minimal tools. Plus, leaving your modern conveniences behind and using only what nature provides allows you to escape from your normally hectic life, offering a bit of peace and mindfulness.

GEOCACHING

Geocaching or treasure hunting with GPS is a way to combine adventure, exploration, nature, and technology. Using GPS coordinates, participants search for strategically placed hidden caches. This modern-day treasure hunt can take you to interesting places you might not discover otherwise. It's a great family activity that can be adapted for all ages and fitness levels. It encourages physical activity, problem-solving, and creativity while enjoying the great outdoors. You'll also become a part of the geocaching community, giving you a new social outlet for your new outdoor skills.

WILDLIFE TRACKING & IDENTIFICATION

Another way to deepen your connection with nature and learn a practical skill to help you survive in nature is wildlife tracking and identification. As you learn to recognize animal tracks, signs, and behaviors, you'll gain insights into local ecosystems and wildlife habitats. Not only will this make hikes and nature walks more engaging, but you'll also be able to identify and track animals in survival situations to find water or hunt for food. You'll also find that your observational skills become sharper as you become a more active participant in the wilderness instead of just a passive observer.

CONCLUSION

Now you know that sitting on the toilet doesn't have to be boring—you can actually learn a thing or two while taking a "number two!" But don't let this be the end of your toilet education. Keep a book full of facts or even an encyclopedia in the bathroom to continue learning about things you probably didn't learn in school.

After all, you're in control of what you do in the bathroom, so why not take the time to learn what you really want to know, or at least interesting things that you wouldn't have known otherwise? Sure, you could use your phone for that purpose—especially if you're one of the 65 percent of people who bring their phones with them to the bathroom—but let's be honest, that's a little gross, considering you probably don't sanitize your phone as often as you should.

Instead, keep this book or another one in the bathroom for the express purpose of learning while on the pot. It will be just as enlightening as anything you can find on your phone—and much more sanitary!

Made in United States
Cleveland, OH
06 December 2024